I enjoy sharing my books as I do my friends, asking only that you treat them well and see them safely home

D. J. Emick

NO HIGHER HONOR

the story of MILLS E. GODWIN, JR.

by M. Carl Andrews

NO HIGHER HONOR

the story of MILLS E. GODWIN, JR.

by M. Carl Andrews

BOOK LAYOUT AND JACKET DESIGN
BY CARL E. LARSON

THE DIETZ PRESS, INC
RICHMOND, VIRGINIA

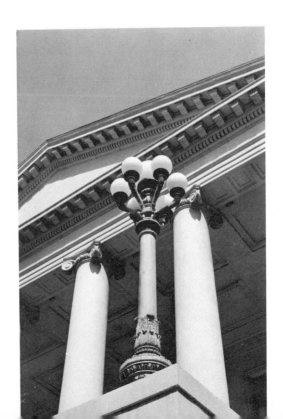

TO BECKY

CONTENTS

CONTENTS

ix

There are many advantages in having reached that venerable state of a long-term observer of the public scene. And one of the most distinct of these is to have had the opportunity of identifying those you believed to have the potential of top performers and seeing that judgment verified by subsequent events.

Such a case is that of Mills E. Godwin, Jr., whom I first knew as a 33-year-old member of the House of Delegates. The brightness of his star was not then fully apparent, but there was no mistaking the fact that the General Assembly of 1948 had welcomed into its midst an unusually capable, vigorous and enterprising young member destined to go further than the lower chamber of the State Legislature. As the leaves of the calendar turned with the seasons and the months lengthened into years, the Godwin story began to unfold into one of the most interesting sagas of Virginia.

Many have attempted to define and classify the basic characteristics of successful men and hardly any two have offered the same, or even similar, answers. But to me one of the outstanding traits of Mills Godwin is his remarkable ability to gauge public sentiment and to guide it into constructive channels of his own molding. His timely championing of major improvements in education, coupled with the inauguration of the sales tax in Virginia, is but one example of the sagacious application of this sixth sense.

It is good that this book is being written by another experienced observer of Virginia politics and government, immune to the bias that admittedly rests with me as an assistant for the four years of the Godwin administration and a friend of much longer duration. Some may say that by reason of this I peer through rose colored glasses. No doubt I do. These Godwin years have been both strenuous and exhilarating, and if these words show the pleasure I have reaped by virtue of being a part of them, this is as I would want it to be. And perhaps the impartial judgment of my ex-colleague of newspaper days, M. Carl Andrews, can be better evaluated in the light of these obviously prejudiced paragraphs.

No comparable period in the story of occupants of Virginia's Executive Mansion has been filled with so much drama, accomplishment and pathos. This is told in vivid detail in the ensuing pages, carefully documented by extensive research and convincingly portrayed by reason of the author's success in capturing the human element, so often hidden in the recitation of history. Those many years Carl Andrews spent as a newsman and editor were but a prelude to his best work, "No Higher Honor".

Williamsburg, Virginia

Carter O. Lowance

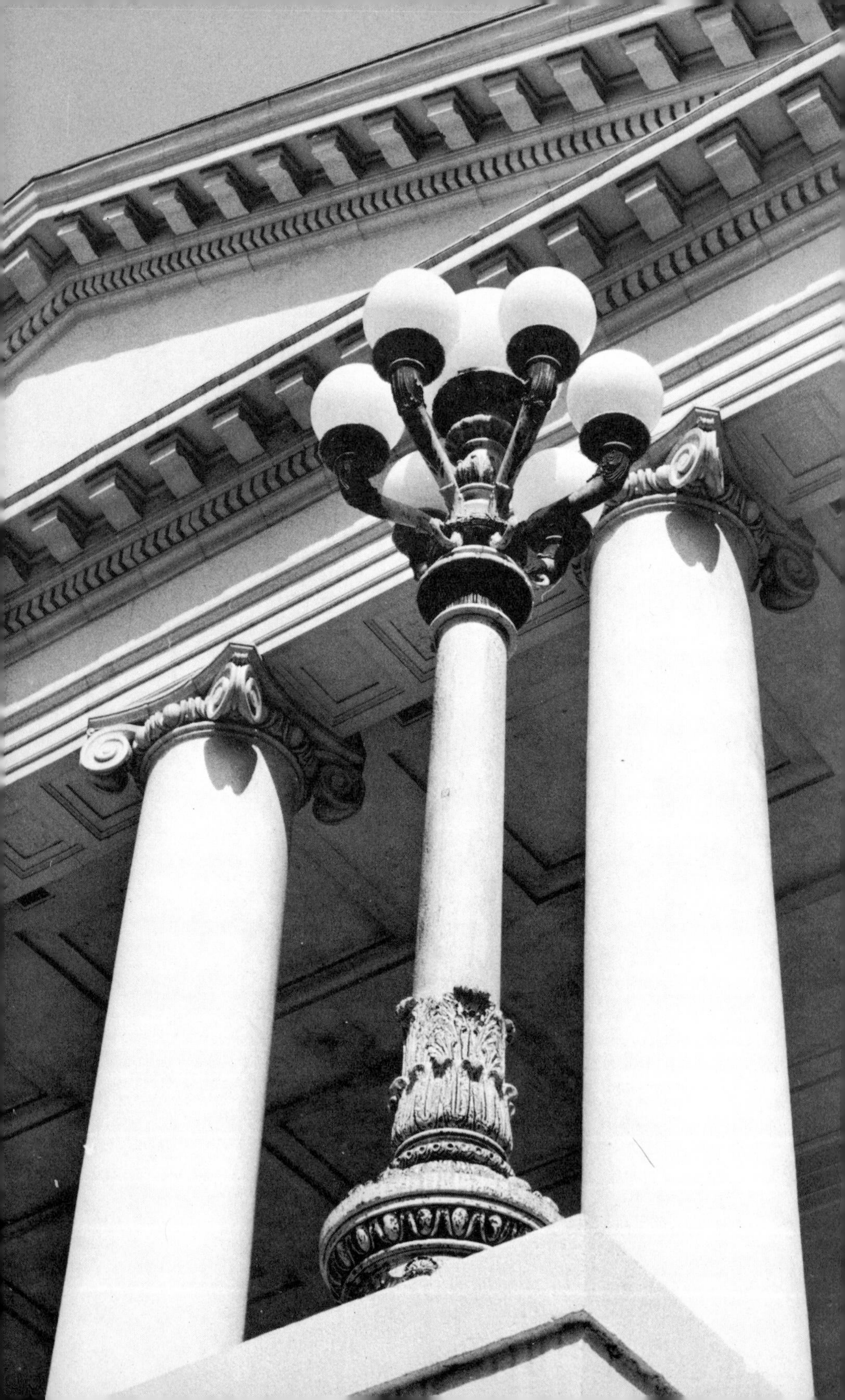

PREFACE

This represents the first attempt, at least in this century, to produce a book dealing with the life, times and record of a Governor of Virginia immediately upon the close of his administration.

The extraordinary impact of the Godwin Years upon the framework of government, upon the institutions of the Commonwealth, upon the industrial and economic growth of the State and, indeed, upon the lives of the people, seemed to call for an effort to preserve the story while it was still fresh in mind.

The invitation which came to me from Richard S. Gillis, Jr., executive director of the Virginia State Chamber of Commerce, presented both a pleasant challenge and a rare opportunity although the erection of such an early publication target date as March 1-15, 1970, had its alarming aspects.

My retirement from editorship of The Roanoke World-News editorial page November 1, 1969, provided just three months for concentrated effort in assembling material, researching, holding interviews and doing the actual writing.

Very fortunately, both Governor and Mrs. Godwin somehow were able to find time during those last busy weeks of his administration to sit for frequent interviews to provide background material on electronic tape. This included a weekend at the Mansion during which we discussed many personal details.

I am deeply indebted to the Governor and his gracious and charming First Lady for their invaluable assistance. Provided with an outline of questions, he was able, by utilizing available spare moments, to set down in great detail the more important events of his political life, especially the gubernatorial years, and even a wealth of hitherto untold personal stories.

To my knowledge, no Governor ever has had time or taken time to make such a record. The tapes have been of tremendous help in assembling this book. Indeed, so valuable do I consider them that it is my intention at the proper time to place them in the Virginia State Library so that future historians may have access to them.

Luckily for me and for this record, Mills Godwin possesses the rare gift of almost total recall. Although his recollections required checking in newspaper files and mircofilms as well as other sources, I never once found him in error.

Much of this record is his personal story, as it should be, and his account of events, particularly as to behind-the-scenes political operations, is fascinating, at least to an editor who knew him and watched him operate most of his 22 years on Capitol Hill either in the General Assembly, as lieutenant governor or as Governor.

Grateful acknowledgement is made to Carter O. Lowance, Mrs. Pat Perkinson and John Wessells, of the Governor's staff, for their assistance in assembling material, as well as to the many who have contributed through interview or letter.

No effort is made here, of course, to recount every detail of legislative action in the four years because space would not permit. Rather, we have touched those things which have signalized Virginia's unparalleled transitional period.

I must be frank to admit that I already had well-defined ideas about Mills Godwin's place in history before the invitation came to write about it.

My research, study and personal look into the record has served to confirm the opinion that he must be ranked with Harry F. Byrd in naming the outstanding governors of modern times.

Indeed, in many respects, he deserves to be placed foremost among those who have led Virginia and helped it achieve a new measure of the greatness which marked the formative years of our Nation.

This is, in no way, a reflection upon those other Virginians who have served their state in their time, each doing with what he had and with what the people were willing to provide.

Any number of titles might have been given this work such as "The Metamorphosis of a Governor" or "A Virginian for His

Time" but, in the words that every occupant of the office has employed, there is "No Higher Honor" than the governorship.

Mills E. Godwin, Jr., certainly a Virginian who rose to leadership at the right time, has been a superb politician whose intuition and sense of timing are nothing short of amazing.

The first Governor to be elected by a mere plurality, he knit the people together as few predecessors could do and left office universally admired, respected and trusted.

This is the story of a man who went through remarkable change from massive resister to school integration to become little short of patron saint of education from grade school to college.

It is the story of a man who was raised in the Byrd Organization with all its conservative fetishes, who saw the need of the hour and led the way in abolishing the sacred pay-as-you-go system through enactment of the sales tax and passage of an $81 million bond issue for capital construction at colleges and mental hospitals.

It is the story of a man who persuaded his State to banish the fears and political neuroses which had beset it since Reconstruction days and, however belatedly, enter the Twentieth Century.

It is the story of a man who did not hesitate to adopt new ideas simply because somebody else suggested them first.

It is likewise a story of triumph and tragedy, of joy and pathos.

It is the story of a man who, in my opinion, is far from having completed his service to Virginia.

He will be remembered and deserves to be remembered for having ended the stultifying pay-as-you-go system, for establishing a fine Community College system which brought the Jeffersonian dream to the people, for guiding the state's great industrial and economic growth and finally for projecting what is virtually a new Constitution of Virginia.

I but echo the words of hundreds of citizens who have commented since they heard that this book was in production when I say that Virginia is fortunate to have had him.

M. CARL ANDREWS

Roanoke, March 1, 1970

*Defining the horizons of a new era:
Mills E. Godwin, Jr. delivers his
inaugural address.*

THE GODWIN POLITICAL PHILOSOPHY

Labels as applied to one's political philosophy are often misleading because they mean different things to various people.

I am a realistic conservative. My philosophy of government is basically conservative in fiscal affairs, and perhaps moderate in relation to those services, and to the extent thereof, that government ought to provide for its citizens.

I reject a liberal classification as generally understood by today's standards.

I try to be a realist and also an advocate of responsible progress. I have long maintained that in government the status quo cannot, and it ought not, be maintained. Seldom does a State stand still. If it does not move ahead, it surely will move backward.

Government as we know it in this country was never designed to do everything for us. Someone told me early in my public service that the true test of every public servant was to know how much money to ask from the taxpayers in order to provide the necessary and essential public services that government ought to provide. To some degree many public officials will not submit to this test.

I do not believe that I stray from my conservative convictions when I encourage our people to provide quality public and higher education for all of the young people of Virginia, adequate and modern mental and public health programs and facilities, responsible welfare efforts, good highways, and other proper services. But these things should be provided within the limits of available revenue and without placing unreasonable and burdensome taxation on our citizens.

A well-bundled crowd on the Capitol's south portico listens to the Godwin inaugural.

NEW ERA FOR THE OLD DOMINION

I, Mills E. Godwin, Jr., do solemnly swear that I will support the Constitution of the United States, and the Constitution of the State of Virginia, and that I will faithfully and impartially discharge and perform all the duties incumbent on me as governor, according to the best of my ability, so help me God.

With the recitation of those words of the traditional oath by the tall, dark-haired, handsome young lawyer from tiny Chuckatuck down in Nansemond County—an area whose Indian names still speak eloquently of the beginning of the nation—a new era opened for the Mother of States.

Surrounded by senators, congressmen, former governors and state officials, Godwin receives the oath from Chief Justice John W. Eggleston.

None of the half-frozen thousands shivering in the stands in front of Thomas Jefferson's noble Capitol or the other thousands watching on television or listening by radio all around the Commonwealth could know what lay ahead, but the next four years were destined to be the most progressive and eventful since Harry Flood Byrd, Sr. stood there forty years before almost to the day and promised a new era of action.

It was January 15, 1966 and the General Assembly—oldest law-making body in the Western Hemisphere—had been in session three days waiting for Gov. Albertis S. Harrison, Jr. to bow out and his lieutenant governor, Mills Edwin Godwin, Jr., to take over and outline his program.

The mercury of the thermometer hovered at 30 degrees and there were occasional snow flurries as the crowd gathered. When, if ever, has there been a pleasant inaugural day in Richmond? Spectators joked that maybe the event should be postponed to June like the birthday of Britain's monarchs and just let the Governor assume office on the appointed day.

Gov. and Mrs. Harrison emerged from the front door of the 153-year-old Georgian Mansion for the last time. The Governor pocketed the keys which have passed from one occupant to the next for nobody knows how many years. They got in a yellow convertible, swung around the circle with the swan fountain, drove out of the Capitol grounds past the statue of George Washington on horseback, surrounded by other great Virginians, and moved on to the John Marshall Hotel where they picked up Gov.-Elect and Mrs. Godwin, as tradition demands, then came back to the Capitol.

Virginia inaugurations are always good shows and as such gathering occasions for the state's ex-governors, senators and representatives in Congress. There was a vacant place and a noticeable one—for the first time in almost a half century Harry Byrd, Sr. was missing but his son, Harry, Jr., was there, newly appointed to the U. S. Senate seat of his father.

There were former Governors Colgate W. Darden, Jr., William M. Tuck, Thomas B. Stanley and J. Lindsay Almond, Jr., Sen. A. Willis Robertson and all ten congressmen from both parties.

The only incongruous note in the quadrennial spectacle was

2

offered by a group of college students bearing placards touting State Sen. Henry E. Howell, Jr., of Norfolk, for U. S. Senator. State Sen. William B. Spong, Jr., was destined to win that seat from Robertson in the days ahead while Howell was to be a devisive influence in the Democratic Party's old time solid front, often at loggerheads with the incoming governor.

One by one Chief Justice John W. Eggleston and other senior members of the court gave the oath of office to Atty. Gen. Robert Y. Button, Lt. Gov. Fred G. Pollard and finally to Governor Godwin. Around Capitol Square National Guardsmen fired the traditional 19-gun salute.

Quietly by custom, the Harrisons disappeared into the Capitol and then out a side door, entered their waiting automobile and were off for a home at Lawrenceville which had seen them very little in four years, leaving the center of the stage to the new Governor.

Mills Godwin came to office the first governor in history to be elected by plurality rather than a majority as the result of a political row which carried over from the Lyndon B. Johnson—Barry Goldwater presidential battle of 1964.

Feelings growing out of that campaign ran deep and bitter with result that the Democratic vote was seriously split. William J. Story, a hard-line reactionary, ran as the candidate of the Virginia Conservative Party and compiled over 75,000 or 13. per cent.

This enabled A. Linwood Holton, Republican, to press Godwin and prevent him from obtaining a majority. The final count showed Godwin with nearly 270,000 or 47.9 per cent compared to Holton's 212,000 or 37.7 per cent. Another 1 per cent had gone to George Lincoln Rockwell, the later assassinated Nazi.

Remarkably under the circumstances, Godwin managed to pull labor, farmers, business and other elements together for a comfortable 58,000 lead. It was a new experience for Virginia but he came to the governorship with high hopes and bright promise of getting the state moving.

It is an emotional moment in the life of any man when he is sworn into office as governor and suddenly feels for the first time the full weight of responsibility he has been seeking so diligently and now has realized. This was the hour for which

3

Mills Godwin had spent nearly two decades in preparation. He was to be pardoned a slight show of nervousness.

With all the foresight of an experienced hunter and fisherman, he had donned thermal underwear beneath the stylish morning clothing. The word got around and a lot of other officials and spectators wished they had emulated his example.

Keeping the customary amenities to a bare minimum, the new Governor proceeded to deliver the shortest inaugural address on record—just eleven minutes in which he set the tone for an administration of action and leadership toward new horizons in education, economic progress and human relations.

Not once did Godwin mention the words "sales tax" although everyone was aware of what outgoing Governor Harrison had proposed when he submitted his budget for the 1966-68 biennium and knew that his successor would offer his own version to the General Assembly in joint session two days later.

He spoke reverently of "Virginia's Golden Age of two centuries ago", recalled the service of devotion by forebears, their sacrifices and their warning against centralized power.

Now the 68th Governor of Virginia under the Commonwealth, Godwin's mind went back to the 148 other men who had preceded him in that position since Queen Elizabeth I bestowed the title on Sir Walter Raleigh in 1584 before Jamestown. With a mind which dotes upon history, he undoubtedly ticked off many of the names as he awaited his call to duty—courageous John Smith who kept the colony alive—Patrick Henry, Thomas Jefferson, Edmund Randolph, Henry Lee, James Monroe, John Tyler, Sr. and Jr., Fitzhugh Lee, Harry Byrd and perhaps even William E. Cameron, the last Republican governor in 1882-86.

Certainly there flashed across his mind the name of Richard Bennett, the only other man from Nansemond County to serve as governor when he was elected by the House of Burgesses in 1652-55. Illustrious company.

As a follower of the Byrd Organization which pulled Virginia from the mud, starting in 1926 and built sound, honest government on a paying, no-debt basis, he recalled that in the election just past the people had demanded that their dreams of schools, colleges, hospitals and highways be brought to reality.

He chose to begin with education. "Knowledge is the great

4

equalizer of our time", he declared. "With it come all the fruits of life . . . if there is a main root to the excesses and to the inertia which get in our way, if there is a handmaiden to poverty and failure, it is ignorance. Let us marshal our resources against it".

Therein lay the determination to launch a Community College system, to strengthen existing institutions of higher learning, to promote the public schools and elevate teacher pay.

The people, he said, were expectant.

"We make a mistake, as their leaders, if we get too far ahead of our people. But we make a greater mistake if we fall behind them. I have made a compact with myself that my own errors will be in the former category. I would be accused of having too much faith in the people of Virginia, rather than too little".

The inauguration over, the frozen paraders passed in review along the narrow drive which skirts the South portico. After a short pause for lunch, the new Governor and his wife were back at the Capitol for the reception dictated by custom.

There they were joined by Lt. Gov. and Mrs. Pollard and Atty. Gen. and Mrs. Button together with Chief Justice and Mrs. Eggleston and House Speaker and Mrs. E. Blackburn Moore.

Such receptions have become too big for the Mansion where they once were held. Now the long line of well-wishers stretching out to the front gates of Capitol Square slowly filed past the famous Houdon statue of Washington and beneath the marble gaze of seven other Virginia presidents and Virginia's first honorary citizen, the Marquis de Lafayette.

Enthusiastic Becky, 12-year-old daughter of the Governor, stood as much as she could and then waited until at last the new First Family was home for dinner with their immediate families and their first night in the Mansion.

There was to be no doubt about the leadership of Virginia for the next four years. The farm boy from Chuckatuck had come a long way. Not only that, but he knew where he wanted to go and where he desired to take his state. He was ready to put 18 years of experience in the General Assembly to work and, as events were to prove, Virginians were ready and willing to lend him a hand.

Birthplace: In this comfortable farm house overlooking the Nansemond River Mills Godwin was born Nov. 19, 1914. Except for the television aerial it has changed little.

A HERITAGE IN PUBLIC SERVICE

Until he entered public life, Mills E. Godwin, Jr. paid scant attention to genealogy although he was aware that his ancestry went back over 300 years within the confines of the two small counties of Nansemond and Isle of Wight on the south side of the James River.

Indeed, it was not until 1961 when he was running for lieutenant governor that those who enjoy tracing lineage and drawing family trees began to dip into the past. That task, as is usually the case with old Virginia families, took them back to England.

The name itself antedates the Norman conquest of 1066 and is derived from two Saxon words—"God" (meaning good) and "wine" (meaning friend). It was found in Cambridgeshire, Shropshire, Norfolk and Oxfordshire in a census of 1273. Members of the family appear to have been landed gentry or yeomanry.

The Governor gets a chuckle from the citation by one researcher that the famed heroine of a ride au naturel through the streets of Coventry, Lady Godiva, was the wife of Earl Godwin, the local bigwig interested in imposing oppressive taxes. He does not, however, claim her as an ancestress.

There was a Thomas Godwin in Buckinghamshire in 1440 and this is worth remembering because the same name appeared in Virginia almost exactly 200 years later.

Which was the first Godwin to set foot in the New World is unknown although a Samuel Goodwin was among the first to be slain by Indians at Jamestown in 1607.

Listed in the company of the ship Abigail in 1620 was Reinould Godwin who apparently joined the colonists. Daniel Godwin settled in Charles City County in 1635, Devereaux Godwin in Northampton in 1637 and John Godwin in Isle of Wight in 1647.

John Godwin probably was the progenitor of the clan in Isle of Wight and Nansemond, although there is no way to prove

7

it, and most likely was father of the original Col. Thomas Godwin.

In the early days of the colony there was not much time for record keeping in families. Here and there a family Bible survived but for the most part records were maintained at Jamestown and later at seats of the shires or counties. Unfortunately, fires often destroyed such papers as existed, notably at Jamestown.*

The first of four generations of Thomas Godwins, the first two bearing the rank of colonel, appeared as burgess from Nansemond in 1654-58. He was sheriff of the county and a vestryman in the Chuckatuck Parish, dying in 1713.

Either he or his son of the same name was Speaker of the House of Burgesses in 1676, the same year Nathaniel Bacon staged his ill-starred rebellion against the royal governor. They owned land on the west branch of the Nansemond River.

Which side Speaker Godwin favored we do not know but we do know that the second Col. Thomas Godwin commanded the militia in his area, got into an argument with Gov. Francis Nicholson over the governor's asserted right of induction, and was removed by Nicholson in 1705. He was presiding justice of his county at his death.

The third Thomas Godwin continued the tradition by serving as burgess from Nanesmond in 1714 and 1723 and was sheriff in 1731-34. His son, Joseph, was burgess from Isle of Wight in 1723 and sheriff in 1719.

A little known fact is that the Quakers gained substantial foothold in this part of the colony in the latter half of the 17th Century and it is recorded that the brothers Thomas (3) and Edmund belonged to the Chuckatuck Quaker Meeting House in 1682. However, they shifted to the Established Church and both were vestrymen between 1702 and 1709.

The name of Mills entered the family when Edmund wed Mary Mills. He died in 1755 leaving two sons, Jonathan and yet another Thomas.

This Thomas, whose will was probated May 13, 1779,

---

* Considerable information in this chapter is drawn from the Virginia Magazine of History and Biography, Vol. 5.

fathered the first Mills Godwin, who died in 1826. This Mills Godwin's daughter Ann Gray (1786-1856) married James Holladay whose name is borne by the Godwin family farm today.

Following the American Revolution in which numerous Godwins served, one as a lieutenant, others carried on the tradition of public service. From then through the Civil War their names are to be found as justices of the peace and as members of the State Senate and House of Delegates from Nansemond, Isle of Wight and Norfolk Counties.

It was no surprise, therefore, that Mills Edwin Godwin, Sr. should be interested in politics or that early in life his son should seek to follow in his footsteps and emulate the examples of a distinguished ancestry.

"Bud" Godwin acquired his nickname as a farm boy.

BOYHOOD IN THE COUNTRY

There is no more wonderful place for boyhood than the farm and it would be difficult to select a better spot than Holladay's Point Farm where Mills Edwin Godwin, Jr. was born Nov. 19, 1914, the only boy among three sisters.

It is a big farm of 500 acres, 300 under cultivation and the remainder in woodland, fronting over two miles on the north side of the Nansemond River near its confluence with the James and Hampton Roads.

The farmhouse, adequate but not huge, stands among a grove of trees, overlooking the broad expanse of water, the bank sloping down to marshes near the waterline with a pier jutting out for use of boats which transport produce to market.

9

Nansemond River, flowing past the front door, was center of attraction and recreation for the boy Godwin.

It was here that young Mills' father had come at the age of 14, an orphan from Isle of Wight, to live with an uncle. Farming had been in the blood for generations and he soon took over the management as well as serving as father to four younger sisters, seeing to it that they received education although he never managed more than four years of schooling.

The farm lies but three miles from the tiny town of Chuckatuck (an interesting, Indian name said to mean "crooked creek") and it was there that Mills, Sr. met Otelia Darden, native of Nansemond who had attended Farmville State Teachers College —now Longwood College—and soon married her, ending her teaching career. It is interesting to note that years later the son followed his father's example.

When Mills, Jr. was born he already had two sisters, Mary Lee and Mildred Elizabeth. A third, Leah Otelia, arrived four years later. Their father saw to it that they attended Farmville and all three graduated to become teachers.

Tom Sawyer and Huck Finn never had more fun than young Mills on the farm. Of course, there were chores to be performed. But there was plenty of time for other things.

In season, when the watermelons and the truck crops were ready for market, the boy accompanied his father and some of the Negro farmhands to Suffolk, Norfolk and Portsmouth or occasionally to Newport News, there making acquaintance with the world outside the farm.

"Mine was a happy childhood", he loves to recall. "There was always something to do. I never lacked for playmates. There were ten colored families who lived and worked on the place and plenty of children. I loved baseball and basketball. Few white boys lived anywhere near and I never saw them unless they came to visit or I had the chance to visit them.

"So I played with the colored boys and we had a wonderful time. I guess I was going on 12 before I realized that there was anybody else."

These experiences instilled in him a lifelong respect for and admiration of the Negro. Today only one of the families remains on the old farm which is operated on lease but every visit is a happy time for colored friends around Chuckatuck.

There was harvesting and hog-killing to occupy time but the river out in front of the house was always beckoning adventure. Young Mills and his playmates went out in the family boat just to explore, to fish or to tong for oysters. He built a fish trap and was proud when he could supply a meal. Even as governor he has continued to make fishing one of his chief forms of recreation.

No American farm boy should grow up without learning to hunt and to use a gun properly and this Mills learned from his father. He still enjoys hunting when he can find the time.

Memories came flooding back to his mind as we visited the old homeplace on the day of the Democratic runoff primary last August.

It was "old home week" all over again as we entered the village firehouse with its red engine, shining like new.

The judges—78-year-old Mr. Chapman, his daughter, Mrs. Bradshaw and Mr. Thompson—greeted the governor as the home town boy he was, known to all as "Bud".

The ballot box is an old metal drum about three feet in length and perhaps 14 inches in diameter, bearing the name of a business firm in fading letters. Metal "feet" have been soldered on to keep it from rolling off the table. Nobody knows how old it is or where it came from.

Mr. Chapman took time to tell with a hearty laugh about the big presidential election when the drum was full of ballots and more flooding in. He pressed a new garbage can into service and flabbergasted one lady by telling her that the ballot box was full so he'd just have to toss her vote in the garbage!

Over at the old farm things looked normal.

The big red barn is still there as well as other buildings, the machinery shed and the smokehouse. The concrete and brick horse drinking trough is broken now because tractors have replaced the faithful old mules.

There is still a metal basketball ring on the barn door. The pier out front is disintegrating. After the highway came through in 1929 and a bridge was built across the Nansemond, linking the area with Suffolk, Portsmouth and Norfolk, the need for water transport had ended.

It was a comfortable life. There was running water in the house and the acetylene lamps by which the future Governor and his sisters studied long ago gave way to electricity.

With a school teacher mother and a self-educated father with a passion for learning, the Godwin children never had any doubts about school.

There were no school buses in those days and so Mills and his sisters drove the three miles in a surrey over dirt roads, often muddy, to the consolidated school in Chuckatuck. On cold days Otelia Godwin wrapped them in blankets and occasionally there was a heated brick or stone to keep the feet warm.

Like so many rural citizens, Mills Godwin, Sr. acquired a Model T Ford which negotiated country roads with determination and success for years. Then, in 1926, he demonstrated affluence with purchase of a Reo and the children were allowed to substitute the old Ford for horse and surrey with Mary Lee proudly driving.

Children of today's generation who wail about lack of parking spaces around schools scarcely four or five blocks from home will find it hard to believe that schoolyards only a few years ago needed parking space for horses and buggies with hitching posts and watering troughs.

A comparatively young Governor, leaving office at 55, remembers it very well.

SCHOOLDAYS IN RURAL VIRGINIA

Mills Godwin, Sr. was becoming more and more prominent in the affairs of Nansemond County. After serving on the School Board several years, he stood for the Board of Supervisors in 1931, was elected and served 12 years until forced by ill health to give up. He was also a lifelong Democrat and when Harry Flood Byrd became governor in 1926 the elder Godwin was one of his strongest supporters. He became one of the founders of Ruritan National in 1930.

As a matter of fact, young Mills—then just 10 nearing 11 —got his first political impressions from the 1925 primary fight between Byrd, using the Cardinal as his emblem, and G. Walter Mapp, employing a map of Virginia, as they campaigned for the nomination. Byrd won the race on a "pay-as-you-go" platform for highways and the Godwins, father and son, were faithful Byrd followers from then on.

It was in 1927 that Mills Godwin, Sr. decided to move from the farm into Chuckatuck where there were better accommodations— school nearby, country store close at hand and the church just on the edge of town.

Godwin's first cousin, Charles B. Godwin, Jr. had been elected Commonwealth's Attorney of Nansemond and convenience demanded that he live closer to the office in Suffolk. His huge old family home—two stories with half basement and large

13

attic—located in the heart of the tiny town, was now available. Mills and Otelia Godwin moved in with their three daughters and son.

Home in Chuckatuck: Here young Godwin moved with his family at age 13, remaining until his marriage in 1940.

The house still stands, erected in the 1890's with round tower and big windows on one side, wide porches front and back, the half basement always cool in summer and warm in winter, the attic big enough for regular living use. It sheltered the parents until their deaths in 1945 and 1946 and watched the children grow to adulthood. The second daughter, Mildred Elizabeth, continues to live there with her husband, Ray Virginius Knight.

Mary Lee (deceased 1953) became a school teacher like her sisters, wed William J. Jones, principal of the school at Whaleyville, also deceased, leaving three children—William J., Jr., Mills Godwin and Webb Darden, all college graduates, the last two holding Ph.D. degrees and the youngest now in his junior year at the Medical College of Virginia.

Leah, the youngest, married Gordon Stanton Keith, and they live in Chesapeake, having two daughters, Kay Godwin and Betty Stanton.

The high school years in Chuckatuck were happy ones for young Mills. With so many other boys nearby or attending the school, he could enjoy his favorite sports, baseball being his first love. He knew all the big league players and could recite batting averages, fielding averages and club standings. Although not "any sort of athlete", in his words, he nevertheless made both the baseball and basketball teams. He also engaged in other school activities including debate and public speaking at which he early proved highly adept.

"I was just an average student", he recalls. "I really can't say that I over-applied myself. I wasn't valedictorian, although I did manage to finish first among the nine boys in the senior class. As I recall, all the girls finished ahead of us".

Nevertheless, he was a leader and class president.

Some of his fondest recollections are of the little school of probably not over 200 pupils and its faculty.

—Photo courtesy Mrs. Dorothy J. Griffin

Schooldays: Eleven-year-old Mills Godwin is second from right on second row in this group picture of grades 4-7 at Chuckatuck Elementary School in 1925. Lillian Griffith Turner was his teacher.

15

There was, for example, F. H. "Cutie" Christopher, the principal who had graduated at the College of William and Mary at Williamsburg just across the James from Chuckatuck. Christopher and his wife, also a teacher, lived across the street from the Godwins. Known as a "tight disciplinarian" who ran a good school, he was a close friend of the elder Godwin, by then a school board member, and pointed the younger Godwin for William and Mary. He remained at Chuckatuck 25 years before moving on to a bigger job at Franklin. He and his one-time pupil, the Governor, remain on friendliest of terms.

Of his grammar school teachers, the one Mills Godwin remembers best and who is one of three credited by Godwin as having a great influence on his life, was Mrs. Annie Shreeves, who lived at nearby Crittenden. She was a stern disciplinarian but loved the English language and, says the Governor, "I owe her for much of the English I know. I recall that she used to require us to memorize a new Bible verse every day and when we memorized a whole chapter we had to recite that. Thanks to her, I still can recite many parts of the Old and New Testaments".

Fortunately for the Governor, reading of the Bible, like prayer, had not been banned from the public schools in those days.

Then, there was Will N. Rippey, an Iowa native and graduate of the University of Missouri who moved from Hanover county to Chuckatuck in 1929 as teacher of vocational agriculture, remaining until his retirement and death in 1967.

Rippey probably had as much political influence on the early career of Mills E. Godwin, Jr. as any other person. He recognized the boy's ability, entered him in an oratorical contest of the Future Farmers of America, a contest Mills won, and sought to encourage him toward politics.

Gradually, young Godwin developed into a polished speaker and was frequently in demand at high school and in his church. It was Rippey who predicted that he would be Governor one day.

"Rippey", recalls the Governor, "was a rabid amateur politician who enjoyed participation in campaigns, who exulted in triumphs of his men and grieved at their defeat.

"I never shall forget the night in November, 1948, when Harry Truman came from behind in the early morning hours to beat Tom Dewey. We were listening to radio and as the tide turned, Bill laughed so hard he got down and rolled in the floor".

It was during this period that young Godwin emerged into leadership of the Oakland Christian Church, a sect strong in Eastern Virginia which later merged with the Congregational Church and they in turn with the Evangelical and Reformed Church to form today's United Church of Christ.

He headed the young people's group, frequently spoke in Sunday School, later became teacher of the Men's Bible Class, a position he held until going to the Governorship, as well as chairman of the Board of Deacons. After college and before marriage he was president of the Eastern Virginia Sunday School Association, a large assembly of his church people.

"Religion", he says, "has always played a deep and abiding place in my life".

It is good that this is so because it was to sustain him in one of the darkest hours which can come to any man, turning the sweetness of success into the bitterest dregs of personal tragedy.

Vacation time: Bud Godwin was 13 and dressed in knickers and Argyle sox of the day when he visited the Ocean View amusement park and sat for this postcard picture.

In October, 1929, the great worldwide economic depression finally reached the United States. Collapse of the Stock Market touched off a chain reaction which reached down gradually into every phase of life in America. Those who lived on farms were far more fortunate than their city cousins. At least they ate.

But when Mills Godwin, Jr. was graduated from Chuckatuck High School in June 1931, the depression's effects were proving devastating on the farm. What produce that could be sold went for less than cost. Crops rotted in the field. Merely keeping his own family and seeing to the livelihood of his Negro tenants proved a great burden for Mills Godwin, Sr., who suffered heavy financial reverses.

Mary Lee and Mildred Elizabeth were still at Farmville but soon were able to complete their work and start teaching. For young Mills, however, it was a different story. Vanished was the bright hope of enrolling at William and Mary that fall—there was no money for board and room although tuition in State-operated colleges was virtually free.

Quietly and determinedly a partial solution was worked out in family councils. The boy, still two months short of his seventeenth birthday, was to go to Norfolk and live in the home of an aunt, Mrs. Alice Godwin Barham, while attending classes at the Norfolk Division of William and Mary (later to become Old Dominion University) and earning what he could at odd jobs.

It was a typical Virginia solution whereby those more fortunate stuck by their kin, assisting as much as they could in spanning the rough places of life. It was regarded far more as a privilege than as a duty or obligation. Only those acquainted with the ways of old Virginia families can wholly understand.

A year later things had improved enough at home that young Mills could realize his ambition and transfer to William and Mary in Williamsburg.

September, 1932, found him established in Tyler dormitory, one of the oldest on the campus, its chief advantage being that it was next door to the refectory, known as Trinkle Hall in honor of Gov. E. Lee Trinkle, who "found" state funds to erect it after the old dining hall burned. Getting to meals was a cinch for late sleepers at Tyler and for Mills, who was partly working his way as a student waiter.

His love of athletics sent young Mills, by now six feet one inch in height but still rail-thin, out among candidates for basketball and baseball. It was mostly intramural sport although he did make the baseball team and played first base.

Again, as he modestly describes it, he was "just an average student although I did manage to make the Dean's list during my junior year". Actually, that takes better than an average student.

Interest in debating and public speaking continued and he joined the Philomathean Literary Society which, with its rival, the Phoenix Society, traced its beginnings back to the beginning of the Nineteenth Century. He did some debating and his deep, resonant voice made him a "natural" for the platform. His quick wit and ability to think on his feet stood him in good stead.

Majoring in government and history, he also took Spanish, a language he liked very much, but also found himself fascinated by sociology and took two courses under one of his favorite professors, Dr. D. J. Blocker. Other faculty members who he recalls contributed much to his education were Dr. J. R. L. Johnson, a master of English language, and Dr. Richard Lee Morton, head of the history department, authority on Virginia history and prolific writer on the subject.

His first year at William and Mary found the boy sharing a room with a young man, seven years his senior, who was something of a nonconformist. Reserved, kind and considerate of Mills during the week, he was something else on weekends.

Prohibition was still the dubious law of the land but the roommate from Stuart in Patrick County, had his lines of communication with the Williamsburg bootleggers and frequently managed a binge on Saturday night to celebrate surcease from the rigors of academic life. He also possessed a gun in defiance of college regulations and got peculiar enjoyment from shooting out town street lights. He never finished college.

Nearly 30 years later when Mills Godwin, Jr. was running

19

for lieutenant governor he heard that his friend was operating a country store on Rt. 58 near Hillsville and stopped to renew acquaintance.

The man wasn't in the store but was found up on a hillside with a mule, plowing. He recognized the candidate approaching and they had quite a reunion during which Godwin picked up one vote.

Godwin's roommate in the 1933-34 year proved to be Percy Trotman of Churchland, a town near Chuckatuck. Being almost neighbors and kindred souls, they got along well together. Godwin's junior year proved to be considerably less hectic.

With his collegemates, he shared the grief which descended upon the campus when Dr. J. A. C. Chandler, president since 1918, died and was replaced by John Stewart Bryan, Richmond publisher and member of the Board of Visitors.

It was possible then to enter law school without having completed undergraduate work and mindful of family finances in the continuing depression, young Godwin transferred to the University of Virginia Law School in 1934. However, a ruptured appendix operation resulted in loss of most of a year from school and it was not until June 1938 that he received his law degree.

They were years devoted to hard work and far less student activity than in undergraduate days. Once again, he describes himself as "an average student" but he was storing up the knowledge so necessary to creative leadership.

Housing for graduate students at the University then was their own concern and they made out as best they could with rented quarters in Charlottesville. It is a matter of record that Mills Godwin once shared an apartment above a funeral parlor. There was a noticeable lack of noise to interfere with study. He frequently worked at the funeral home and had a list of fellow students who served as professional pallbearers.

In those days it was not necessary to have one's law degree before taking the state bar examination. Godwin passed it in 1937 and was ready for pratice when graduated the next year.

Long before then it had been settled that he would join his cousin, Charles B. Godwin, Jr., Commonwealth's Attorney of Nansemond with offices in Suffolk and enjoying a wide practice when not serving as prosecutor.

It was Charles who had encouraged Mills to pursue the law as a career with the approval of Mills, Sr., who pointed out that farming was becoming more technical and more onerous every year.

The two cousins were most compatible and soon young Mills was a partner in the law firm and assistant Commonwealth's attorney, gaining invaluable experience for years in the General Assembly and in the Governorship.

Charles Godwin practiced law until his death in 1954 and held the prosecutor's post for 25 years without opposition. Personal tragedy entered his life when Charles B., III was killed in a pony jump in boyhood. A second son, James C., finished at Randolph-Macon and Washington and Lee Law School, practiced with his father and cousin, and was appointed circuit judge by Gov. Albertis S. Harrison, Jr., where he now serves.

Mills, Sr. had arranged for his son to buy a blue Ford coupe upon graduating from law school so it was possible for the young lawyer to live at home with his parents in Chuckatuck, driving the 10 miles each way every day.

Fortunately, young Mills had worked during his college year summers as an automobile salesman for another cousin, Bernard Godwin, who owned the Ford agency in Suffolk. He knew what to do when a car needed attention.

The car was to be an important asset in courtship days.

Courtship on the waters of Hampton Roads, summer of 1939. Cousin Charlie Godwin's yacht was ideal vehicle for college student Mills to spark his sweetheart, Katherine Beale.

THE COURTSHIP OF KATHERINE

It was the first day of school in Chuckatuck, September 1937, and Mills Godwin had not yet started back to Charlottesville for his final year in law school.

At such a time there is little to do in a tiny village but the young bachelors as usual were following a local custom known as "looking over the new teachers" at the elementary and high schools, located side by side.

Mills' old teacher and mentor, Will Rippey, was standing with two of the newcomers in front of the schools when he spotted the tall Godwin, grinning from ear to ear, striding across the yard.

"Wait a second", he said to the new teachers as they turned to enter the school, "I would like you to meet a friend of mine— the most eligible young bachelor in Chuckatuck!"

"I'm sure I couldn't care less!" said one young lady, who happened to be engaged.

"Me either!" agreed the other, who happened to be Katherine Thomas Beale, pretty, five feet four and trim of figure with brown wavy hair and flashing blue eyes.

They waited and introductions were performed. Godwin, who had escaped unentangled from coeducation at William and Mary and women graduate students at U. Va., was smitten.

"I really wasn't too much interested" she recalls today, "because I was almost engaged when he came along but he was a most persistent suitor".

He was, indeed. The last year in law school saw him finding frequent excuses to come home. Katherine was boarding in a home across the street and just two doors away. It was a most convenient arrangement.

Katherine Beale was an infant of 21 months when both her parents, in their early 20's died the same night during the awesome influenza epidemic which swept the United States and much of the world in 1918 during World War I. She does not remember them but visits to their graves always leave the same impres-

22

sion. "They were so young!" she exclaims.

Katherine was the Fenton Beales' only child. She was taken into the home of her paternal grandparents, Mr. and Mrs. Thomas Beale, in Southampton County and her father's sister, Mrs. W. Emory Beale, became her guardian. After Mrs. Beale's marriage, Katherine and her grandmother moved with her to live in nearby Holland.

Graduating from Holland High School, Katherine went on to Harrisonburg State Teachers College (now Madison College) and was planning to continue her education in graduate school. She had, however, changed her major from history to elementary education because the state was crying for more teachers.

It was Hugh White, superintendent of Schools, who insisted on sending her an application and September 1937 found her in Chuckatuck ready to teach the third and fourth grades.

"The persistent suitor" found many things to do during courtship although Chuckatuck was so tiny it did not even boast a movie theatre.

By now there were good roads to Norfolk, Portsmouth, Suffolk and Richmond and a bridge over the James to Newport News. Mills took Katherine to movies and stage plays. He liked "live" theater best although not a concert fan, and she recalls that they drove in the blue Ford to see "Oklahoma!" at the Richmond Mosque.

There were frequent church picnics and socials—although a Baptist, she joined his Church, Oakland Christian—and when plays were staged there or at the high school he often took a part.

They were active in his church and by now he was such a persuader and exerted such a magnetism upon youth that many in the community urged him to enter the ministry.

Charles Godwin owned a fair-sized motorboat which classified as "yacht" since it could sleep six comfortably. The young couple enjoyed many a cruise on the James, Hampton Roads and Chesapeake Bay with Godwin and his wife as chaperones and hosts.

For entertainment at home there was radio, of course, for it was the era of big network shows such as "Lux Radio Theatre" and regular programs by the great stars—Jack Benny, Fred Allen, Amos and Andy, Fibber McGhee and Molly—and we must not forget the regular broadcasting of the great dance bands —Paul Whiteman, Sammy Kay, Gene Kruppa, Jack Teagarden, Glenn Miller and a host of others.

It was an age of wonderful music and entertainment which in many ways was superior to television of today but is unknown to a younger generation.

Katherine and Mills were married on Oct. 26, 1940 and a new two-story brick house was started under his father's supervision while they were on their honeymoon. After living with his parents in the old home, they moved into their new house on Jan. 16, 1941.

It was a good, substantial house and cost $7,500. Ruefully the Governor recalls that a small addition, a garage and paving the driveway cost considerably more than that in 1956.

It was to be a short occupancy, however, because in December that year the Japanese struck Pearl Harbor and like every other patriotic young American, Mills Godwin immediately started to seek the best means of serving his country.

Honeymoon House: Here, in a new home built under the watchful eye of Mills Godwin, Sr., the newlyweds moved in January, 1941. War was to make it a short tenure.

For anyone living in proximity to the vast military installations around Hampton Roads, the thought of routine life while the nation was at war was intolerable.

Late in 1942 Mills Godwin, Jr. went to Norfolk and, in a burst of inspiration, applied at the same time for a commission in the Navy and for appointment as a special agent of the Federal Bureau of Investigation which was seeking young attorneys for counter-espionage work.

The Navy physical examination disclosed existence of a sinus cyst and need for surgery which was performed in Suffolk. While he was recuperating, the chief agent of the FBI in Norfolk showed up and asked him to report immediately. This was early 1943. He accepted and went to Quantico for training. Within a week the Navy offered a commission but it was too late.

After 16 weeks of training at Quantico and in Washington at the FBI Academy, he was assigned to St. Louis where Mrs. Godwin was able to join him. Because of his mother's illness, he was transferred to Norfolk and the young couple was able to reopen briefly the honeymoon house in Chuckatuck.

Following his mother's death in 1945, Godwin was shifted to Richmond and remained there until separation from the service in December, 1945. Mrs. Godwin had returned to teaching during the emergency at the old Chuckatuck school while he was in Norfolk on temporary assignment.

As far as Mills Godwin is concerned, there was little extraordinary or fantastically adventurous in the FBI years. He disclaims any James Bond incidents or anything very exciting, although he was proud to receive two commendations signed by J. Edgar Hoover for especially meritorious work. If there was any lasting impression from the FBI years it was a strengthening of his respect for authority of the law and the necessity for its fair and impartial enforcement. It was yet another good foundation stone for building a career in government.

The transition from war to peace was not difficult. The old

law office was waiting in Suffolk and there was the task of settling down in a home which had seen them all too little. Charles Godwin, after the death of Mills, Sr. in 1946, became like a substitute father and brother to the young partner. He retired as Commonwealth Attorney in 1947 and the two enjoyed a wonderful association until his death in 1954.

Life in Chuckatuck was calm and pleasant. Everybody knew everybody else in the village and for miles around.

Next door to the young Godwins lived the Henry Grady Norfleets and their daughter, Trudy Eva, whom they watched grow up as though she was their very own, attend Madison College like her mother, Nelle Austin Norfleet, and become a school teacher. Norfleet has always watched over their home when they were away. The rose garden between the two homes became simply "our rose garden" to both families.

On the other side lived close friends, Alec and Dorothy Moore, who raised a family of five. Now a widow, she has been teaching at Old Dominion University.

Into an apartment across the street after World War II moved A. Gordon Brooks, his wife Polly and daughter Betsy, then two years old. Brooks came as principal of the high school and remained two years before moving on to Brookville near Lynchburg, thence to Roanoke's Jefferson Senior High School and to Botetourt County as superintendent, and then to Richmond as director of the Division of Teacher Training in the State Department of Education. The two young couples became fast friends, drawn even closer together by awesome tragedy within the Godwin household in the summer of 1968.

It was inevitable that one so well known by now and respected not only in Chuckatuck and Suffolk but throughout Nansemond—an accomplished speaker and one seemingly born to be a leader— should be called upon for public service.

Godwin became at various times chairman of the Suffolk-Nansemond County Red Cross chapter, of the American Cancer Society, the March of Dimes, the Tuberculosis Association and the Community Fund.

He joined his father's Ruritan Club—second in the country, served as President in 1948, was named Zone Governor in 1949, District Governor in 1950, Vice President of Ruritan National in 1951 and President of Ruritan National in 1952. He rose to senior warden of the Chuckatuck Lodge AF&AM and was a Pythian and Moose. He was also a member of the Rotary Club in Suffolk.

Dr. I. W. Johnson of Suffolk, who served the Oakland Christian Church as pastor for 52 years and who was among the oldest Godwin friends, was also a rare oddity—president of the Bank of Whaleyville—and soon Mills found himself on the board of that thriving little institution which he still serves as vice-president.

It was in this period that he became teacher of the then adult Bible Class (later men's class) a post he held for 25 years and was elected to the Diaconate of the Church.

For services like these he twice was designated as "First Citizen" of Suffolk and Nansemond and it was small wonder that so many friends urged him to go into politics. Theirs was not a too difficult task because undoubtedly he had entertained visions of following in his Cousin Charles' footsteps or even standing for the General Assembly.

At the time there didn't seem much chance of getting into the House of Delegates. The Nansemond-Suffolk seat was held by Willis E. Cohoon of Suffolk, strong cog in the Byrd Organization and highly popular with his fellow legislators in both houses, with a strong following in his home bailiwick.

Finally, after taking stock of his own popularity around the county and in the city and having consulted all the angles with his Cousin Charles, Mills Godwin determined to make his bid.

In serious mood yet happy over the prospect, he hurried home that evening to inform Katherine. A modest, retiring person, she loved the quiet life and the prospect of getting involved in politics shook her little world.

Looking back at the turning point in their lives, she recalls 22 years later "my first tears of married life were shed that day".

Young Mills was astonished as he looked into her brimming eyes.

"What's the matter, honey, don't you want me to run?" he asked.

"I just want you to be a good country lawyer!", she wailed.

Smiling today, she says: "I relented because I firmly believe

27

that a good wife should want what her husband wants to be happy and have a contented life".

Katherine Godwin had no way of knowing it then, but her husband was taking his first step toward the Governor's Mansion.

Future governor and U. S. senator: State Senators Godwin and Harry F. Byrd, Jr., long close friends, confer on an important point during a General Assembly session.

LAUNCHING OF A POLITICAL CAREER

The announcement of Mills E. Godwin, Jr. that he would oppose such a stalwart of the Byrd Machine as Willis E. Cohoon took old line conservatives by surprise but the campaign quickly developed into a real horse race.

The Godwins, too, were staunch Byrd supporters so there was no conflict of political ideology. Rather it was a contest of personalities and Cohoon was to discover that while gaining popularity at the State Capitol he had neglected fences around the farms and in the villages of Nansemond.

Godwin's platform presence and polished speaking performances prevailed—he carried every precinct in the county and won by better than 1,200 although trailing Cohoon some 500 in Suffolk.

Admittedly green, Delegate-elect Godwin went to the Capitol late in 1947 to ask the veteran Col. E. Griffith Dodson, House clerk, about seating arrangements and assignments.

"To this day I remember what Colonel Dodson said in response to my approach: 'Young man, we are glad to have you here— we operate under the philosophy 'The King is dead— long live the King!'

"I quickly discovered that I had ruffled the feathers of the leadership when I challenged and defeated one of their favorites. Speaker Alvin L. Massenburg, of Hampton, gave me less than the best committee assignments. I discovered that so far as I was concerned, 'the King' wasn't doing very well."

Opening of the 1948 session—last of Gov. W. M. Tuck's administration—found Godwin not fully accepted and he was slapped on the wrist with such committee assignments as Insurance and Banking and Chesapeake and Its Tributaries.

An unwritten rule of the House is that freshmen members should be seen as little as possible and heard not at all. However he may have yearned to participate, Freshman Godwin had the good sense to keep still. Without significant committee assignments, he found it difficult to keep occupied.

Delegate Godwin took it in good grace and waited for his opportunities. One came on the fight over Tuck's proposal to boost income taxes in order to increase teacher pay. As the son of a teacher, the brother of three and husband of another, the man from Chuckatuck knew whereof he spoke and his eloquence was persuasive. This and the support of other administration bills earned him Tuck's gratitude.

But just as things were looking up there came the spirited four-way Democratic primary of August 1949 with Sen. John S. Battle, the Organization candidate, opposed by Horace H. Edwards, Richmond attorney and legislator, Remmie L. Arnold, the Petersburg pen manufacturer, and Col. Francis Pickens Miller, idol of the rising liberal faction.

Edwards, an Isle of Wight native, was related to some of the Godwins and Mills Godwin found himself committed to the Edwards cause early in the game. As the campaign progressed it became evident that Edwards was losing support as indicated when influential newspapers withdrew from his camp and swung to Battle in hope of turning back the Pickens Miller bid. Nobody worried about Arnold, who eventually ran a very poor fourth.

Godwin was among those who urged Edwards to pull out of the race in favor of Battle but his back was up and he refused. When the votes were in he had carried but four counties and two of them were Isle of Wight and Nansemond where Godwin had run the show. Battle turned back Miller by substantial margin but for Mills Godwin it had been a very unhappy political experiment.

Early in 1950 Godwin went to Gov. Battle's office, explained his situation and offered him the utmost support of his program. Battle was grateful, considerate and granted the Delegate from Nansemond-Suffolk numerous favors but that failed to help matters much in Godwin's House standing on its committees.

It was not until the 1952 session that Speaker E. Blackburn Moore, of Berryville, gave him better appointments and selected him for a place on the Virginia Advisory Legislative Council, that all appeared at last forgiven.

Floor Leader Roy B. Davis of Halifax was not showing much enthusiasm for his post and it was Edmund T. DeJarnette, the acting floor leader, who recognized Godwin's talents not only for speaking but for compromise and pulling hot chestnuts from the political fires when necessary.

There is no way of telling how far Del. Godwin might have gone in a fourth term had not fate intervened to engineer another tack for his career.

During the early autumn of 1952 Democrat Adlai Stevenson was engaged in a vital campaign with Gen. Dwight D. Eisenhower, the Republican's hope of winning the Presidency for the first time since Herbert Hoover left office in 1933.

Addressing a Stevenson rally in Southwest Virginia, Lt. Gov. L. Preston Collins, of Marion, was fatally stricken. A special session of the General Assembly was impending for the purpose of redistricting legislative seats and it was necessary for state authorities to move fast.

The Democratic State Central Committee met and endorsed Sen. A. E. S. (Gi) Stephens, of Smithfield, to succeed Collins. Forewarned of developments, Del. Godwin announced almost simultaneously for Stephens' seat from the 5th District encompassing Nansemond, Isle of Wight, Southampton and the cities of Suffolk and Franklin.

Gov. Battle summoned a special election for a date which proved advantageous to Godwin. No opposition developed and he was elected.

Coincidentally, Willis Cohoon ran without opposition for his old seat, held the past six years by Godwin. The wounds of the 1947 struggle long since had healed and they remained good friends until Cohoon's death several years ago.

A new area of service had opened for Mills Godwin when the 1952 special session convened in December for emergency reapportionment of the General Assembly.

Young Senator Godwin in typical speaking pose.

MAKING HIS MARK IN THE SENATE

It is an unusual thing for any legislator to serve in both houses of the General Assembly in a single year but the special session for redistricting in December 1952 made it possible for Mills Godwin to achieve that distinction when he moved over to the Senate after spending the regular session in the House.

Whereas he had been prevented by political circumstances from achieving any true distinction as a delegate, things were destined to be considerably different in the Senate.

One of the most powerful figures in the Byrd Organization was the veteran Sen. Charles T. Moses of Appomattox and it so happened that he was Mills Godwin's uncle by marriage, he having wed a sister of Mills Godwin, Sr. years before. Moses took Godwin under his wing and helped see to it that he got better committee assignments.

A fortuituous circumstance also was that Lt. Gov. Stephens was grateful for the fact that Godwin had persuaded Willis

Cohoon not to seek Stephens' Senate seat after Godwin had taken Cohoon's place in the House.

In the next eight years Sen. Godwin found himself serving on the Governor's Budget Advisory Committee, the Virginia Potomac River Commission of which he was chairman and the Commission on Constitutional Government as well as top Senate committees—Finance, Courts of Justice, Counties, Cities and Towns, Fish and Game (Chairman) and Welfare.

An unusual circumstance was to make him a marked man almost at once in the special session. It was necessary, following the 1950 U.S. Census, to realign districts more fairly in proportion to population. For some senators like Charley Moses this meant tremendous expansion of his district to include urban areas he did not wish to cultivate. He feared a shift of voting power which could separate him from his seat. As a matter of fact, he made it plain during debate that in his opinion country votes should be worth more than town or city votes. The hand which guided the plow, turned the soil and grew the crops had more inherent right to guide the ship of state than the hand of an office worker or a factory employe, he avowed. It was an attitude that had its inception with the rise of the first towns in colonial Virginia.

Consequently, in the closing hours of the session, Senator Moses staged a one-man filibuster. He brought out the Code of Virginia and other law books. He read from old books dealing with government. He recited election returns of years gone by, He discussed almost anything that seemed relevant and a lot that didn't.

At first, the rest of the Senate enjoyed the show and members from the House even came across to hear what seemed a good joke. Charley was well beloved and many shared a feeling for his rebellion. After three hours, however, it was no longer funny. Christmas was not far away and some House members were threatening to press for adjournment.

It was at this point that young Senator Godwin recognized an opportunity. Addressing the lieutenant governor, he asked if Senator Moses would yield. A bit winded by this time, Uncle Charley agreed. Godwin then moved a 15-minute recess and requested that Moses join him in the Clerk's office.

There, just off the Senate floor, Godwin suggested that Moses was waging a losing battle, that he had made his point but that passage was a foregone conclusion. Reluctantly, Moses agreed, realizing that in so doing he would be giving his nephew a popular leg up the ladder of legislative achievement.

The Senate reconvened, Moses announced that he had been talked into withdrawing his opposition and the bill passed. The next morning the Assembly adjourned with leaders of both houses and Governor Battle acclaiming Godwin for sterling work. He was on his way.

Godwin's first full session in the Senate, 1954, proved to be one of the most eventful and tumultuous that body had witnessed in many years. Thomas B. Stanley, moving down from the House in Washington, had just come to office after defeating State Sen. Ted Dalton, Republican, by an uncomfortable 43,000 majority.

As a matter of fact, it wasn't anything that Stanley did to give the Democrats their worst scare since Reconstruction days, but Dalton's proposal late in the campaign for a $100 million bond issue to build highways. This brought Senator Byrd into the fight and turned the tide.

Stanley had been elected on a "no tax increase" platform yet proposed in his inaugural address a one-cent boost in the gasoline tax to help carry through the state's highway building program. The fur flew then and continued to fly throughout the session but undoubtedly the most amazing development, so far as Byrd leadership was concerned, was the rise of the "Young Turk" movement.

Godwin had actively campaigned in many parts of Virginia for Governor Stanley, both in the primary and in the general election, and for the first time was fully accepted in the Governor's Office and became one of the leaders on the administration team.

Led by such progressive, youthful figures in the House as Armistead L. Boothe of Alexandria, Stuart B. Carter of Botetourt, Joseph E. Blackburn of Lynchburg, George M. Cochran of Staunton, Walter A. Page and Toy Savage of Norfolk, Kossen Gregory and Julian H. Rutherfoord, Jr. of Roanoke, E. C. Compton of Greene County and William B. Spong, Jr. of Portsmouth, the Young Turks, working within the party, vowed to "drag the Organization into the second half of the Twentieth Century". They comprised a not inconsiderable portion of the House and exercised strong persuasion over the remainder.

Best described as progressives rather than as liberals, they were not rebels in the sense of the 1960's. Rather they sought a liberalization of attitudes by the party leadership that would loosen purse strings of the state especially for schools and school teachers. Denied attention in committees, they took their fight to the floor.

This was the picture in the final days of the 1954 session when the Turks were managing to hold up the budget bill. Their idea was to eliminate the $7 million allocated for return to the taxpayers under the Automatic Tax Refund Act of Sen. Harry F. Byrd, Jr. They wanted this applied to teacher pay increases.

Midnight Saturday marked the end of the legal 60 days prescribed in the Constitution for legislative sessions but the impasse continued. Tempers were growing short on both sides of the Capitol. There were threats of political reprisals if somebody didn't yield. Time after time the clocks were set back an hour—an ancient dodge of pretense which technically, at least, makes acts of the Assembly lawful.

Four times the Speaker and Lieutenant Governor appointed

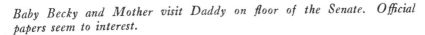

Baby Becky and Mother visit Daddy on floor of the Senate. Official papers seem to interest.

conference committees to iron out the dispute, with the Young Turks in House control holding out against the Senate. The session went into Sunday morning, then afternoon and night.

In the Senate, Godwin had been supporting the Administration position all the way. Finally, when a fifth set of conferees was appointed, he was among them and he wasted no time in trying to put his persuasive powers to work for compromise. The Young Turks still wanted a big slice out of the Byrd mellon but the Senate would not hear of it. After lengthy dispute, the conferees agreed on a $2,125,500 allocation to go to teachers. The House surprisingly accepted rather promptly.

Taking the floor to defend the compromise in the Senate, Godwin called on all his eloquence but was turned down by a scant two vote margin. Impasse again with the Senate recessing and the House threatening to adjourn.

It was at this point that E. R. Combs, the Senate Clerk generally regarded as spokesman for Sen. Harry F. Byrd, Sr. on matters of political and legislative policy, told some of the leadership that a compromise must be reached.

Word went down the line and when the Senate reconvened it was an administration stalwart, Sen. Landon R. Wyatt of Danville, who moved to reconsider the vote on the conference report. The Senate then reversed itself and, by a narrow margin, gave the House and the Young Turks what they wanted.

It is natural that in the wake of this event Senator Godwin should have some second thoughts and wonder whether or not he might have injured his political career by advocating and achieving compromise with the rebel faction. Actually there was no aftermath. He continued to enjoy growing recognition and to pick up more important committee assignments.

But something else had happened that was to have much greater significance. This was the opening of the first faint crack in the solid facade of the political House of Byrd. Two years later, the Byrd Automatic Tax Refund Act, popular in its conception but tending to stultify in practice, was repealed. The Young Turks would get slapped down more than once but they had learned that it was possible to buck the Organization for good cause and, as events proved, the winds of change were stirring however faintly.

36

INTEGRATION AND SCHOOL CRISIS (1954-1960)

It was on May 17, 1954 that the U. S. Supreme Court handed down its historic decision in the case of *Brown vs. Board of Education,* directly affecting four Southern school districts but reaching into every part of the Old South as it ended forever the Separate but Equal doctrine which had stood since 1896. Virginia was never to be the same again and the fight which ensued was to split the Democratic Party from top to bottom.

What follows is vital to the story of Mills Godwin because he was a staunch disciple of Sen. Harry F. Byrd's "Massive Resistance" and because he represented a senatorial district with some of the heaviest Negro population in the state. Nansemond, his home county, had 65 per cent, Isle of Wight 52, Suffolk 37 and nearby Southampton 61 per cent.

Looking back at the period of desperate maneuvering during which Virginia tried every legal avenue of subterfuge and defiance, Godwin makes no apology for his part.

"No man could have survived in public office, especially in Southside, if he was 'soft' on integration", he says.

Gov. Thomas B. Stanley had been in office but four months and J. Lindsay Almond, Jr. was attorney general when the blow fell.

Bravely but naively, Stanley endeavored to accept the decision in stride with a prediction that moderation would prevail and that the state would work out its destiny. He did not reckon with the temper of the white population and most certainly he did not consider the reaction of Byrd in Washington.

Very quickly the lines began forming. On one side there were those who accepted the Court's decision as "the law of the land" and vowed compliance. On the other side were those who swore defiance, non-compliance and last-ditch resistance to racial integration of their schools. As it turned out, there was no middle ground.

The balance of 1954 and the big portion of 1955 were consumed in marshalling forces. Senator Byrd asserted firm control

37

while Stanley strove desperately to maintain some semblance of reasonable direction.

Uncompromising opposition centered in the Fourth and Fifth congressional districts lying along Virginia's southside and including Senator Godwin's district. Spearheading the opposition was the newly formed "Defenders of State Sovereignty and Individual Liberties". Arrayed against them, determined to see the Court's ruling enforced was the National Association for the Advancement of Colored People with growing local membership and well heeled with funds from outside the state.

Casting about for some solution which might hold up in the face of court pressure, Governor Stanley named a special all-white committee, headed by Sen. Garland Gray, an arch-segregationist from Waverly in the heart of the Black Belt.

The Gray Commission's report, delivered in November 1955 and hardly surprising, practically admitted that some integration was inevitable but urged that no child be compelled to attend an integrated school. It suggested pupil assignment on the basis of aptitude, health, the availability of transportation and similar factors with local district control. A system of tuition grants was advanced as an alternative.

A special legislative session which followed (November 30, 1955) posed the question of a referendum on a limited constitutional convention. Subsequently a referendum yielded an approximate 2½ to 1 majority favoring tuition grants which would enable parents to send their children to private non-integrated schools.

The 1956 regular session of the General Assembly, midway of Governor Stanley's term, distinguished itself largely by adoption of a futile resolution embracing the doctrine of Interposition.

Dug from beneath the dust of 150 years by James Jackson Kilpatrick, editor of the Richmond News Leader, Interposition asserted the right of any state to place its sovereignty between its people and the power of the federal government. First asserted by John C. Calhoun, South Carolina statesman and vice president of the U. S. (1825-32), during the great congressional debates in the 1830's and 1840's, it had been given the death blow by the Civil War. About all its resurrection could do now was to encourage the battle against integration and help gain time. For a brief, frantic period, the rest of the South looked hopefully as Virginia gave it a whirl. They were doomed to disappointment.

In conference with Senator Byrd and others of the Virginia delegation in Washington, state leaders planned their next move and then took a breather while everybody went to Chicago for the National Democratic Convention.

At Chicago, with former Governor Battle as spokesman, they again became embroiled in an argument over the party loyalty oath and narrowly escaped excommunication by a convention which nominated Adlai Stevenson for a second try against President Eisenhower.

They came home fighting mad at the National Party, most of them helping Senator Byrd maintain his "golden silence", and pitched into a special General Assembly on August 27 to see what could be done about the Gray report.

Governor Stanley preceded the session by ditching most of the report and offering his own Massive Resistance plan, including a pupil assignment system, setting up a three-man state board to review all applications for enrollment and requiring the Governor to withhold funds and order schools closed in districts where the federal courts intervened.

Senator Gray virtually assured passage of the Stanley plan when he took the floor to concede that the plan worked out by his committee could not succeed.

After a five-day recess for hearings, during which supporters of both sides besieged the Capitol, the Assembly reconvened September 5 and by the 23rd had completed the program's passage interspersed with a melange of local bills offered by unanimous consent. On September 29, Governor Stanley signed the various measures into law.

This was Massive Resistance at its flood tide and all efforts to preserve local discretion on integrated enrollment were turned back. Senator Godwin as floor leader carried the Byrd forces into a Pickett's Charge of impending doom. In his mind, it had to be done.

"Until the courts knock down this package of bills there

39

Hold the line! Young Senator Godwin states his case.

won't be any integration anywhere in Virginia", he told his colleagues.

Summoning all his eloquence, he termed integration "the key which opens the door to the inevitable destruction of our free public schools" and a cancer "eating at the very life blood" of the system.

The legislation was destined to remain in effect little more than two years or only as long as it took to get cases before the United States and Virginia Supreme Courts.

Having gotten a running start as attorney general, J. Lindsay Almond, Jr. captured the Democratic nomination for governor and went on to defeat Sen. Ted Dalton, making his second effort, in November 1957. As a voice of moderation, Dalton appeared to have a good chance but was crushed in November after President Eisenhower sent federal troops into Little Rock to integrate the high school.

Almond took office in January 1958 and in September came the test cases. Schools in Warren County, Charlottesville and Norfolk were shut down on his orders pursuant to the 1956 emergency law. Prince Edward, center of resistance, continued its defiance. Another rash of private schools began to appear, relying on gifts and tuition grants.

Governor Almond and Atty. Gen. Albertis S. Harrison, Jr. determined to make a test before the Virginia Supreme Court of Appeals in a case styled *Harrison vs. Day* (State Comptroller).

The verdict wasn't long in coming. On the same day in January 1959 the State's high tribunal and a special three-judge federal court sitting at Norfolk held both the school closing and fund cutoff provisions unconstitutional by both federal and state standards.

Result of this was an immediate special session at which Governor Almond backed water and called for a revision of the tuition plan. He also appointed a new commission headed by Sen. Mosby Perrow of Lynchburg to study the matter during a recess. This body came up with a recommendation for local pupil assignment which passed the House but skinned by in the Senate only when Stuart B. Carter of Botetourt, who had been one of the Young Turks of 1954 in the House, got out of his sickbed, went to Richmond and cast the deciding vote. Shortly thereafter local boards, led by Norfolk, began admitting a few Negroes to former all- white schools.

Like the rest of the Byrd "Massive Resisters", Sen. Godwin went down to grudging defeat and with no apologies then or since. However, it is worth listening to what the Governor had to say in late 1969, a full decade after the back of Massive Resistance was broken:

"The people were wholly unprepared to accept it (integration) and there was no chance of getting them to understand the problems involved. It was months before the Supreme Court spelled out its May 17, 1954 decision and gave details of what it really meant. There was a period of waiting during which nothing happened to cause people's feeling to be weakened to any appreciable extent.

"While I was active in the passage of legislation of this period, especially in the 1956 special session, I have never apologized for the part I played in it. One cannot say now, looking back 14 years at what happened, that if he had it all to go over again he would do exactly what he did at that time.

"It would be correct to say, however, that no member, especially from Southside, could have stayed in the General Assembly, who had not held strong views on integration of the public schools.

"We thought that the problem was fraught with many difficulties as, indeed, time has proved. We realized from the begining that the problem was going to be more acute in those areas with high ratio of Negro population and this has proved to this day to be extremely accurate.

"I have always felt and said, especially in the campaign of 1961 (for lieutenant governor on the Harrison ticket) that this period which was allowed for Virginia to test the legality of its laws and to make the most of its effort to preserve its segregated schools, gave our people time to adjust to what inevitably had to happen".

Recalling that he served as floor leader for Stanley legislation, presided at hearings on legislation and was active in the referendum to change the Constitution to permit tuition grants, Mr. Godwin comments:

"There was every reason to believe that enormous problems would continue in many areas and I cannot say even now a decade later that public education has not been adversely affected because of racial integration.

"I am certain that we waited too long to do some of the things we should have done in earlier years to assure full equality of opportunity in education for our Negro children. That's history and water over the dam. Attempt has been made to right the wrongs. It is my hope that problems now will not be so criticial that they will destroy the educational opportunities Virginia is prepared to give all children, particularly those in the so-called Black Belt.

"Our people today, even in the Black Belt, would be agreeable to accepting 'freedom of choice' (in schools attended). Where you have to take children and carry them to a school of another race in order to achieve some measure of racial balance there is tremendous resentment in white areas and some colored areas.

"A certain amount of racial integration, while tolerated and acceptable to many, is still unacceptable to some. Where white children are put in a room with 80 or 90 per cent colored children it results in friction and lack of support for the public schools. And most unfortunately, better students with affluent families, are withdrawn and sent to private schools, leaving the middle class and poor white children to attend with the colored.

"I think it is worth noting that in this era (1954-60) some of us were designated 'school closers' wanting to destroy public education.

"There has never been any evidence of this because even at the height of the debate more and more money was appropriated to schools. We realized that Virginia could not go forward without public education. It was a necessity for her well-being. At the same time we didn't want to destroy the best quality education we could provide and that is what we were afraid might happen in many areas".

The explanation may not satisfy a great many people yet one who did not know the situation could not possibly be a fair judge of what happened. Circumstances were such that the "law of the land" as interpreted by the nine members of the Supreme Court came face to face with the customs, traditions and aspects of human character developed over a period of 350 years. Anyone was a fool or at best naive to believe that change could be brought about overnight. In addition, Mr. Godwin and his colleagues of the General Assembly hardly can be blamed for refusing to commit political suicide.

There was absolutely nothing hostile to the Negro race in the Godwin actions. After all, he was born among them, raised with them, played with them, worked with them, and to this day enjoys countless friendships among those of his native Nansemond. And as Governor he was destined to appoint more of them to public office than any other Chief Executive of the State.

As for quality education, he was to move forward from the Massive Resistance days to do more for public education, especially on the higher levels, than any predecessor. It may be said that the times changed, which they did, but the man changed, too. He possessed that rare quality of being able to grow with the needs of his State and its people.

Council of strategy. Godwin, center, confers with fellow senators, Charles Fenwick and Dr. James D. Hogood. —Richmond Newspapers Photo

Undoubtedly the chief extracurricular activity of the Virginia General Assembly session which comes midway of a gubernatorial term is (or was until 1968) playing the political game of deciding who is going to be the next Governor.

During most of this century, especially since the administration of Governor Byrd, the game was played almost like musical chairs. The quickest witted man who was able to pull the most strings and round up the most pledges of support within the Legislature usually wound up with the Democratic nomination.

The disappointed aspirants "got back in line", as the saying went around Capitol Hill, and awaited their turn.

Although it was most helpful to have the blessing of Senator Byrd as head of the Organization, it was not always an absolute necessity. Two men failed to obtain the blessing and still won the nomination and the general election—James H. Price in 1937 and J. Lindsay Almond, Jr. in 1957.

Price had such a wide following in various fraternal circles throughout the state that he could not be stopped. Almond, sidetracked once by Thomas B. Stanley, resolved not to let it happen again and got such an early start that nobody else could buck him.

But the outstanding characteristic of the men brought to Virginia's governorship continued to be their background of experience in state government. The Organization had its faults, but foisting untrained candidates with poor capabilities on the voters of the Commonwealth was not one of them.

Beginning with Andrew Jackson Montague in 1902, every governor in the Twentieth Century until 1970 served his apprenticeship in the General Assembly or in some closely related branch such as the attorney generalship.

This was the picture when the Assembly convened in January, 1960, in Governor Almond's midterm, but already there were indications that a fight was impending for the 1961 Democratic primary.

While Almond had capitulated to the pressure of the courts

and had abandoned his role of No. 1 spokesman for Massive Resistance and while conservatives were resolved to hold the line as much as possible, dissatisfaction was mounting and there were strong hints that a moderate or liberal ticket would emerge.

By December 1960 it was clear that both Lt. Gov. A. E. S. (Gi) Stephens of Smithfield and Attorney General Albertis S. Harrison, Jr. of Lawrenceville were determined to seek the nomination. Both were from Southside counties but for many reasons, some of them inexplicable, Organization sentiment swung to Harrison. It was he who had shared the hard work in the thankless task of trying to maintain school segregation. In addition he had been a popular figure in the Senate before becoming the state's chief legal officer.

As early as the January session, Senator Godwin had been approached to run for attorney general and this pressure increased into the summer. He had no interest in the post, however, despite many pledges of support. Instead, he expressed strong desire to stand for lieutenant governor and by autumn it had been agreed that he would team with Harrison.

There remained the problem of getting an attorney general candidate to complete the ticket. About Christmas the choice fell on Sen. Robert Y. Button, of Culpeper, lawyer-farmer-banker, who had been in the Senate since 1945. He had to be talked into running but became an enthusiastic member of the team which adopted a platform centering on business development.

As might be expected, efforts were made to persuade Lt. Gov. Stephens to stand aside but he resolved to stick, especially after moderate sentiment turned in his behalf.

In March, 1961, Sen. Armistead Boothe of Alexandria, whose break with the Organization dated back to the House "Young Turk" days a decade before, emerged as candidate for lieutenant governor on Stephens' ticket. T. Munford Boyd, blind member of the University of Virginia law school faculty, eventually became the opposition's candidate for attorney general.

There now ensued one of the most heated primaries Virginia had ever witnessed in contrast to the cut-and-dried perfunctory affairs of so many years when the main task of the voters was to endorse the slate put forward by the Organization.

While there was strong rivalry between Harrison and

Stephens, the spotlight seemed to dwell on the contest between Godwin and Boothe. The Alexandria Senator had introduced an amendment to the Virginia Right-to-Work law, spawned during the administration of Gov. William M. Tuck. Had it passed, the change would have almost emasculated the law. Godwin defended the law all the way.

More than anything else, Boothe's position on this issue won his ticket the hearty endorsement of the AFL-CIO which gave it strong financial support. As might be expected, the peril in which the law was placed, inspired tremendous business and industrial support for the Harrison-Godwin-Button ticket.

Integration continued to be a live issue and the Negro vote swung heavily toward Stephens-Boothe-Boyd as the NAACP sought to pin the label of "school closers" on the Organization slate.

What probably made the biggest headlines was Stephens' break with Senator Byrd at whom he lashed out in a speech at Winchester, the Senator's home ground. Byrd thereupon released to the press a letter he had received from Stephens, soliciting the Senator's support and terming him truly one of the great Virginians of the time. The disclosure was a rough blow to Stephens.

The poll tax was still in effect and the total primary vote small but the Harrison ticket won without too much trouble. Harrison's own margin was 47,000, that of Godwin 31,000 and· Button's 25,000. Strength in the Third, Fourth, Fifth and Eighth congressional districts gave them margins which could not be overcome in the urban areas.

As customary, the Democrats joined forces after the primary and turned back without too much effort the threat from a Republican ticket headed by H. Clyde Pearson, of Jonesville, with Mrs. Hazel K. Barger for lieutenant governor and Leon Owens for attorney-general.

Sworn into office as lieutenant governor in January, 1962, Mills Godwin was now one of the leading figures of the state in politics and government. A friendship with Governor Harrison, begun in the Senate, ripened and it soon was no secret that Harrison hoped Godwin would be his successor.

The lieutenant governorship is, in Mr. Godwin's own words, "one of the best offices in the state, possessing honor and dignity without power and without too much responsibility except when the Senate is in session".

There was, he likes to recall, "plenty of room to maneuver and to operate" and as No. 2 man, he became a strong right arm to Governor Harrison, making frequent public addresses which always dovetailed with the Harrison program.

True to his promise, Harrison reorganized the state's industrial development office and put it under the governor. Sen. Harry F. Byrd, Jr. who sponsored the necessary legislation, was appointed chairman of the advisory committee and things began to move. In fact, this became the foundation stone of Godwin's exceptional efforts on behalf of business and industry in the next administration.

Much of the general atmosphere in both House and Senate is provided by the presiding officers and Lt. Gov. Mills Godwin quickly put his interest in parliamentary procedure and public speaking to work. Remembering his own experiences at both ends of the Capitol, he went out of his way to hold information and training sessions with new senators to help them "learn the ropes".

Veteran observers of the General Assembly know how thousands of visitors pour through the tiny galleries each session, including scores of high school classes in civics or political science. Most of the impressions they take home are made by the Lieutenant Governor, presiding in the Senate, or by the Speaker of the House. Here was something that came natural to Mills Godwin, a polished speaker and student of history.

Varying his talks daily so as not to bore the Senate membership, all of whom introduced classes from their districts from time to time, he invariably drew upon history to provide a capsule lesson in government, particularly the legislative branch.

Visitors seemed to flock to the Senate and the result was literally hundreds of invitations to make commencement addresses and other appearences at schools throughout the Commonwealth. It is a source of satisfaction to the Governor that in a sense he helped educate many of today's voters.

So passed the sessions of 1962 and 1964, the second being especially harmonious. In fact, it was so staid that Sen. E. O. McCue of Charlottesville once lamented that it had been "im-

47

possible to stir up even one good fight the whole 60 days". The secret, perhaps, was that the Assembly simply resolved under Governor Harrison's direction to live on what it had and spend only such money as was available.

There was a special session in 1964 to enact legislation requiring a "certificate of residency" after the U. S. Supreme Court outlawed the poll tax as a prerequisite to voting in federal elections. Easily passed, the act was foredoomed and was promptly invalidated by the court.

But, as noted at the beginning of this chapter, the midterm legislative session enjoys other uses and Mills Godwin was charting a new course.

High-Level Pow-Wow: Lt. Gov. Godwin goes over to House for a conference with Speaker E. Blackburn Moore, left, and John Warren Cooke, destined to succeed Moore.

—Richmond Newspapers Photo

48

During the 1964 session of the General Assembly midway of the Harrison Administration, Lt. Gov. Mills Godwin operated quietly and with characteristic efficiency to let it be known that he intended to run for Governor in 1965.

As usual, there was speculation and trial balloon launching in the lobby of Hotel Richmond, known for more than a half century as the second home of legislators. Few dared stay anywhere else lest they miss out on some of the maneuvering.

There was only one outstanding possible rival—Sen. Harry F. Byrd, Jr., who by heritage, parentage and training had every right to aspire to the office in which his father became distinguished. He made no open move, however, for reasons best known to himself.

Godwin and the younger Byrd had been deskmates and close friends in the Senate for years but they never really discussed the governorship openly except possibly for an occasional suggestion from one or the other that he hoped they would never be in position of being opposed at the polls. Neither wanted to fragment the party any more than it was at the time, which was becoming alarming enough to old Organization men.

By the time the regular session adjourned in March, 1964, Godwin believed that he had received fairly well committed support from two-thirds of the Senate and was in even better position with House members.

During the special session late that year he made his plans unmistakably clear but meanwhile the Presidential campaign between Lyndon B. Johnson, seeking a full term in his own right, and Sen. Barry Goldwater, was to involve Virginia politics in all sorts of difficulties.

Here it was that the existence of two Democratic parties came into clear focus. Since early in the first term of Franklin D. Roosevelt in the 1930's when he reneged on campaign promises and launched into liberalized phases of the New Deal, causing a breakaway by both Sen. Carter Glass and Sen. Byrd, Sr., there had been a growing coolness among Virginia Democrats for their party nationally.

As a matter of fact, by 1948 when the State supported Thomas E. Dewey against Harry S. Truman, starting a series of Republican verdicts, it had become customary for conservatives to speak of themselves as "Byrd Democrats", meaning that they customarily voted Democratic in state elections but Republican in national elections.

Nevertheless, party loyalty continued to be so fierce and the oath required of candidates for state office so rigid that it was necessary for these candidates to give at least perfunctory support to presidential tickets of the National Democratic Party.

The only leading figure in Democratic state politics who could ignore the whole thing was Senator Byrd, whose antipathy for Roosevelt carried over against Truman and was not allayed either by Adlai Stevenson, John F. Kennedy or Lyndon B. Johnson. Because of his enormous prestige he could keep the "golden silence" so evident after the 1960 national convention. Others were not permitted that luxury if they wanted to run and get elected to statewide office.

Thus it was that Mills Godwin, with an eye on the governorship in 1965, endorsed the Johnson-Humphery ticket in the summer of 1964—not enthusiastically at all because he could discern the widespread sentiment for Goldwater among Virginia voters, but because it was a matter of "keeping regular". He made just one, for him, rather low key speech on behalf of the ticket at Big Stone Gap in October.

That speech, being innocuous, brought no painful reaction, but another gesture was to bring reaction in which he said later, the conservatives "gave me fits" and all because he chose to do a gentlemanly thing.

Mrs. Johnson, making a campaign swing through the South on a chartered train dubbed "The Lady Bird Special", naturally invited political bigwigs along the route to hop on and ride across their particular state.

Mr. and Mrs. Godwin boarded the train in Northern Virginia and Godwin presented the President to the crowd from the rear platform at Alexandria. They then rode to Richmond where Governor and Mrs. Harrison joined the party and where Harri-

Lady Bird won them over. Mrs. Lyndon B. Johnson and daughter Lynda attracted politicians to her Lady Bird Special, including Gov. Albertis S. Harrison, Jr. (left), Lt. Gov. Godwin (background) and Rep. J. Vaughan Gary of Richmond and Third District.

son made a speech of endorsement. The trip ended at Norfolk.

Godwin came in for blistering criticism from the conservatives then and the next year, but he now recalls, this greatly pleased the liberals in his party and "undoubtedly helped me get the nomination without any opposition".

As soon as the Christmas-New Year holidays were out of the way, Godwin felt that he could not delay much longer in making his public announcement. Yet, he did not wish to move without reaching an understanding with Senator Byrd, Jr. He called Byrd by telephone and they agreed to meet early in January at the John Marshall Hotel.

In the privacy of a hotel room, Godwin laid his cards on the table, including commitments from Assembly members but suggested that if Byrd had any doubts it would be wise to conduct his own private poll. According to Godwin's recollection, Byrd admitted having been encouraged by numerous sources to run for governor but had not made up his mind. They parted good friends.

Eight days after their conference, Senator Byrd, Jr. issued a statement to the press, announcing that he had no intention of making the race. The way was now cleared for Godwin except for carrying out a visit more or less demanded by courtesy.

He went to Washington and there made his ambitions and intentions known to the two aging senators, Harry Byrd, Sr. and A. Willis Robertson as well as to Democratic members of the House delegation. He received several outright endorsements and encouragement from the rest.

On January 9 Mills E. Godwin, Jr. announced that he was a candidate for governor subject to the July Democratic primary.

As it turned out, the decision of Byrd, Jr. was a wise one for his own political fortunes which were to lead to appointment to the U. S. Senate seat upon his father's resignation Nov. 11, 1965.

Shortly after Godwin's candidacy was made definite, Del. Fred G. Pollard of Richmond, announced that he was an aspirant for lieutenant governor, supported by a favorable poll.

Godwin now recalls that he neither encouraged nor discouraged Pollard but he certainly sought no opponent for him and was glad when none appeared.

Later these two conferred with Atty. Gen. Robert Y. Button, who agreed to complete the team but with a warning that this would be his last term.

For a time Sen. E. E. Willey, Richmond pharmacist, toyed with the idea of making the run for governor but eventually abandoned it. No other competitors appeared and for the first time in 54 years there was no statewide primary. The Democratic State Central Committee merely certified the Godwin-Pollard-Button ticket and that was it.

There was a lot going for Godwin already. Within a matter of days after his own announcement he had received a pledge of support in ~~...~~ ~~...~~ ..t in the Senate and House with one exception whom he prefers not to mention for print.

Quickly, too, he persuaded Richard S. Reynolds, head of the great Reynolds Metals Co. to join with Sen. Garland Gray of Waverly as co-chairmen of the campaign finance committee.

This was something of a masterstroke since Gray was an old line Organization man and Reynolds was generally regarded as a moderate, even liberal Democrat. It served as something of an indicator of how Godwin intended to mesh the various factions and wings of his party in the coming campaign.

By late summer Waldo G. Miles, Ninth District chairman, had been named general manager of the campaign, J. William Doswell office manager and Mrs. Pat Perkinson, free lance writer, a speech writer and assistant. She later was to become the Governor's administrative assistant.

Suite 370-72 in Hotel Richmond with a lengthy history of housing successful gubernatorial campaigns was leased and Godwin was ready to put his show on the road.

As usual, the Republican Party had selected its ticket early in the year, with Abner Linwood Holton, Jr., native of Big Stone Gap, Harvard Law School graduate, member of his own law firm in Roanoke and loser of several political races on lower levels, as its gubernatorial candidate. Picked to run with him were Vincent Callahan for lieutenant governor and D. Dortch Warriner for attorney general.

As partner of M. Caldwell Butler, the astute Republican House leader, Holton had been emerging as the most logical man to fill the very big shoes left behind when Sen. Ted Dalton of Radford was named to the U. S. District Court for Western Virginia.

Betrayed as a country boy at heart only by the loping gait of his walk, the tall, blond, easily-smiling and sharp debating Holton promised to be a worthy opponent.

It would have been an interesting race just between Godwin and Holton but a third and complicating factor was to enter the campaign.

Die-hard conservatives and massive resisters from the Southside, angry with Godwin for what they considered his forsaking of principle by riding on the "Lady Bird Special" and unable to accept a Republican of any hue, nominated a ticket known as the Virginia Conservative Party, led by William J. Story, former superintendent of schools at South Norfolk.

There now developed what Godwin terms "a real horse race" that went right down to the wire.

To their credit, both Godwin and Holton tried hard to debate what they considered to be the real issues before Virginia —better schools, growth of higher education, improvement of the state's mental hospitals, attraction of more industry and development of trade, especially foreign.

With the Conservatives the big issue was school integration and they were against it. Story promised a return to segregation despite courts and the federal government. It was what the white people of the Black Belt wanted to hear. At the same time, recalls Godwin ruefully, "they forgot or didn't want to remember" the outspoken part he had played in trying to prevent or retard racial integration of the schools.

The rather awesome bitterness in Southside was emphasized by another of those periodic resurgences of the Ku Klux Klan which held numerous rallies and cross-burnings throughout the Southside counties and even at other points in the state.

Nothing better illustrates the political metamorphosis of Mills Godwin than his endorsement by the AFL-CIO and chief manipulators of the Negro vote such as the Crusade of Voters in Richmond and other cities. Only four years before, running for lieutenant governor, he not only was denied this backing but was the target of their sharpest barbed tactics.

Feelings ran high in areas with large Negro vote and the Conservatives' tactics brought Negro boycotts of business.

Nothing, however, caused Candidate Godwin more alarm than the Klan which he hated with passion and frequently denounced. He later was to have a celebrated confrontation with Marshall Kornegay, the North Carolinian operating as grand dragon in Virginia of the United Klans of America, Inc.

Adding to the Democratic alarm was the fact that the Republicans, endeavoring to make up for their lack of outstanding figures in Virginia, brought in outside talent headed by former Vice President Richard M. Nixon, a personal friend of Holton.

54

Story and his Conservatives made full use of Godwin's by-now-famous ride on the "Lady Bird Special" in October, 1964.

As the campaign developed it became evident that there was a "new Godwin" in the field. From one end of the state to the other he proclaimed the need to put Virginia on the high road of progress, emphasizing public schools, colleges and hospitals.

"I sensed that people in every section of the state were ready to move ahead", he says in retrospect, "and it was likewise evident that they were willing to provide the revenue that would be needed". He does not deny that Holton appealed to much of this vote.

The problem was where the money was to come from and already Governor Harrison was wrestling with it as he prepared the budget for 1966-68. The odds were that he would suggest a state sales tax.

"Late in 1965 some fifteen cities had a retail sales tax", Godwin recalls. "It became evident that unless something was done the cities would become so strong that the state never would be able to impose its own sales tax and we would be in a real straitjacket financially".

In the campaign he carefully avoided being opposed to the imposition of a sales tax but said instead that he would not hesitate to ask for new revenue.

"Fortunately for me, Mr. Holton came out flatly against the retail sales tax in late September", comments Godwin. "At the same time he advocated new programs and expansions of existing programs we estimated would cost $300 million.

"My feeling was that this was an irresponsible position for him to take and perhaps he could take it as a Republican candidate because he would likely never have to deliver or perform on promises he was making—I think this was the big, fatal mistake Linwood Holton made during the campaign".

Godwin evidently read the mind of the state aright because he piled up a plurality of 57,000 over Holton and probably would have done much better had it not been for Story. Fully 90 per cent of the vote collected by the Conservative, in Godwin's opinion, was taken from the Democratic Party.

Godwin was not especially impressed with Holton's 37.7 per cent. Although he polled the largest total to that date for a Republican, he was still far below Ted Dalton's 45 per cent against Thomas B. Stanley.

The Governor-elect could not help but acknowledge the power demonstrated by the Conservative Party, however much of a passing phenomenon. In his opinion, it caused the primary defeats of Sen. Robertson by William B. Spong, Jr. and Rep. Howard Smith by George C. Rawlings in the primaries the next summer.

While finding his total "less than I would have liked", Mr. Godwin considered the outcome "a clear, convincing vote from the people of Virginia—it could be called a mandate" and promised to launch his Program of Progress forthwith. He felt that Holton's vote, like his own, indicated that the great majority of the people of Virginia, were ready to move ahead.

For his part, Mr. Holton looked at the results and declared: "The Republican Party has become a stable and enduring force in Virginia politics". Just how enduring he was to prove beyond doubt just four years later.

Victory Jubilation: Happy campaign workers crowd Godwin headquarters on night of his election to governorship. His face tells story as Katherine embraces Pat Perkinson, one of his chief aides.

—Richmond Newspapers Photo

BUILDING THE TEAM:
RECOGNITION FOR NEGROES

Virginia over the years of successive Democratic administrations built up a strong, capable and loyal army of public servants closely akin to civil service with only departmental heads and key officials subject to removal and appointment by the governor.

One of the proudest boasts of the Byrd Organization was always honest government, untouched by a breath of public scandal or suggestion of graft or malfeasance. If there was any one thing which aroused the wrath of Sen. Harry F. Byrd, Sr., it was the hint of any hanky-panky even on the lower echelons of the socalled "courthouse rings" which were the core of the Organization. Woe to the man accused of possessing soiled linen!

As a rule, a new governor has been glad enough to inherit an efficient, working organization. This relieved him of any necessity for a big turnover in patronage and the making of wholesale appointments at a time when he needed to be concerned with the budget, his program and General Assembly relations.

True, during the course of his administration, the average governor makes more than 2,000 appointments and reappointments. He names judges to interim vacancies, subject of course, to confirmation of the next General Assembly session. He chooses members of boards of visitors at 14 four-year colleges, the Community College Board and to dozens of other boards and commissions.

This process is, in Governor Godwin's words, "a tremendous part of the responsibility which rests upon the Governor".

Recognizing that on the whole, Virginia had able personnel in the higher echelons, he made it his policy to continue all those who had a desire to stay. The Harrison appointees were eminently satisfactory and with a very few exceptions he reappointed them if they were eligible for new terms under the law.

Godwin's first order of business even before starting his campaign for the governorship had been to ask Carter O. Lowance, executive assistant to Governor Harrison, to remain on the job.

Lowance had served with every governor, starting with William M. Tuck. During the Almond term he was vice president of the Medical College of Virginia, now a part of Virginia Commonwealth University, for a little over three years.

Terming him "the one indispensable man in the government of Virginia", Godwin later declared: "I know of no other single individual who is so valuable to our state government as is Carter Lowance. He's a man of unquestioned integrity and great capacity. He's a tremendously effective administrator and one whom Virginia can ill afford to lose".

At Godwin's request, the General Assembly in 1966 enacted a statute creating the position of Commissioner of Administration in the Governor's office to which the directors of Budget, Personnel, Engineering and Buildings, and Planning would report directly, relieving the Governor of considerable detail.

As executive assistant to Harrison, Lowance had unofficially many of the same duties, had in the past handled press relations and was noted for writing a spanking good speech whenever the governor needed one, which was frequent.

Gov. Godwin, of course, had Lowance in mind when he asked for the statute and the immediate appointment met with universal approval on Capitol Hill, with the news media and the public.

Also reappointed were L. M. Kuhn as budget director and now relieved of other tasks, and John Garber, director of personnel.

For the other two positions, Godwin had his eyes on experienced men. He pulled T. Edward Temple from the city managership at Danville—a man who had been called one of the top 10 city managers in the nation and was being sought by Richmond and other communities. A William and Mary graduate and former member of its Board of Visitors, he also had experience in college level teaching.

The choice for director of Engineering and Buildings fell on H. Douglas Hamner, VMI graduate and city manager of Hopewell.

One of the few men not reappointed was Joseph C. Hamrick, the state's first director of Industrial Development under Harrison, who had come into conflict with members of the advisory board over policy matters.

Godwin first named J. Eldred Hill, a former assistant attorney general and Virginia Employment Commissioner, to this vacancy but after a year Hill took a much more lucrative post in Washington and he was replaced by J. Frank Alspaugh of Newport News, who assembled a fine staff and has been praised by Godwin as "best in the history of the state".

William L. Heartwell of Lawrenceville was drafted as commissioner of the Virginia Employment Commission, a task involving public relations know-how and an understanding of human relations.

One of Godwin's more controversial appointees has been Otis L. Brown, 33-year-old Albemarle County administrator when the Governor picked him to succeed William L. Painter as head of Welfare and Institutions.

In poor health, Painter asked to be relieved of his onerous duties, a request Godwin honored but kept him on for a year in the role of consultant as well as chairman of the Commission on the Aging, from which job he retired in 1969.

Brown inherited a good many problems with the antiquated State Penitentiary in Richmond and the penal system in general as a result of which he became a target of press criticism. Godwin believes he has done an excellent job, considering the problems with which he has worked. He is very proud of this appointment.

Determined to do something about the ever-mounting toll of lives on the roads, the Governor set up the Virginia State Highway Safety Commission, naming as its head John I. Hanna, an employe of the City of Richmond who came without appreciable increase in compensation because of his dedication to the project.

For many years the name of Levin Nock Davis, secretary, had been synonymous with the State Board of Elections. Now he was retiring and to replace him Godwin selected L. Stanley Hardaway, farmer from Stony Creek and a clerk in the Senate when that body was in session.

Probably the appointment which gave the Governor most

pleasure was promotion to colonel of Maj. Harold W. Burgess whom he named head of the Virginia State Police, succeeding the retiring Col. Charles W. Woodson.

Burgess was a state trooper stationed in Suffolk when Godwin started law practice in 1938 and had worked his way up through the ranks. They had remained friends for 30 years.

"Virginia has the finest state police in the nation", says Godwin flatly. "Their very presence usually is sufficient to maintain law and order and has calmed tense situations in several areas of the state. For that we can thank the quality and the character of the men".

During Godwin's term in office, two of the three members of the State Alcoholic Beverage Control Board left, John W. Hardy by retirement and Warren Wright by resignation. Named to replace them were Archer L. Yeatts, Jr., veteran state employe who briefly worked in the governor's office as executive assistant, and Ralph J. Davis, president of the First National Bank of Luray. John G. Bruce has been the holdover member.

There were, of course, many other appointments, all of whom Godwin takes pride in and who, he believes, have given good service to the Commonwealth and its people.

But it was in a far different phase of personnel selection that Gov. Godwin was to make innovations and to establish precedents which even now are little recognized and lack appreciation among some of the leadership of those whom he sought to elevate in status.

By this is meant, of course, the first conscious and dedicated effort by a Virginia governor in modern times to appoint qualified Negroes to public boards and commissions.

The number is not great when we consider that blacks constitute over 20 per cent of the population of Virginia but by the time he left office Mills Godwin had named between 35 and 40 Negroes to positions of responsibility and honor.

Suffice here to mention eight of the most outstanding:

William M. Paxton, an insurance expert in Richmond, to the State Hospital Board.

Victor J. Ashe, Norfolk attorney, to the Board of Welfare and Institutions. There was some resentment over this choice and one white member told the Governor there would be wholesale resignations. None developed. Ashe's presence is now approved by just about all.

Hillary M. Jones, Norfolk attorney and member of the Norfolk School Board, to the State Board of Education.

Yarborough B. Williams, Jr., principal of Richmond's John F. Kennedy High School, to the State Board of Community Colleges.

James Edward Sheffield, Richmond attorney, former Harvard faculty member, a Boy Scout executive and leader in the Jaycees, to the Board of Visitors of Virginia Commonwealth University.

Elgin Lowe, first appointed by Governor Harrison, from Isle of Wight, reappointed to the Board of Visitors of Virginia State College. Elected chairman by his fellow members.

Oliver W. Hill, Richmond attorney and Roanoke native, to the Virginia Commission on Constitutional Revision.

When Norfolk State College was separated from Virginia State on January 1, 1969, Gov. Godwin named six Negroes among its 11-man Board of Visitors and one of these, J. Hugo Madison, was elected rector by his colleagues.

More Negroes have been added to the State's general employment. A Negro became a state trooper for the first time. Negroes were named toll bridge and toll road collectors and managers of State ABC stores.

This is unprecedented in Virginia history but in Godwin's opinion the recognition was overdue, is a considerable step forward and will be good for the state.

How did it happen that a white politician from the Black Belt could do anything like this? For Mills Godwin it was easy. He had been close to colored friends all his life from boyhood on the farm. He liked them and was willing to recognize merit as well as leadership and other good qualities among them.

Denied the Negro's organized political support in 1961 when he ran for lieutenant governor, he held no grudges and in turn four years later received this endorsement for governor. He promised to help do something to improve their position and he has done so.

"There has not been enough progress in this area to remove the biting criticism from some areas of the Negro community who do not think enough has been done", he says in retrospect. "They feel excluded from high paying jobs but I do not believe in making appointments because of race, because a man is black or white. I do think that merit and qualification must be the factors that govern our decisions.

"I would be the first to recognize that perhaps we had not done enough along this line in the past. But I don't think that you can 'rebuild Rome in a day' or correct all things that need to be corrected in this matter in one short term of four years. My contention is that the list of Negro appointments in my administration has been an impressive one".

Of all the appointments a governor must make, those which worried Mills Godwin most were the judgeships, especially on the Supreme Court of Appeals. Mrs. Godwin noticed this throughout their tenure of the Mansion.

As circumstances would have it, he made more judicial selections than any other governor, including three to the Supreme Court—former Gov. Albertis S. Harrison, Jr. to succeed C. Vernon Spratley of Hampton and Alex M. Harmon of Pulaski and George M. Cochran of Staunton to succeed Chief Justice John W. Eggleston of Norfolk and Justice A. C. Buchanan of Tazewell.

"There is nothing more important that a Governor does", he says, "and I am proud of these selections".

In a way, it is a great compliment to a governor that judges choosing to retire do so between sessions of the Assembly, thus giving him a free hand. Almost invariably the legislators sustain his choices when they meet again.

In the normal process for choosing judges, they are first nominated at a caucus of the Democratic members of House and Senate, then elected in open session. Quite obviously, no Republican is ever named. The process is not likely to be any different under Governor Holton who might like to get some political balance on the bench but lacks the votes in the Assembly to back him up.

There were three factors invariably considered by Gov. Godwin in arriving at his selections for judges—sentiment of the local Bar Association, sentiment among legislators from the district and opinion of leading citizens. Sometimes, not often, he picked men not on the list.

Judges, he declares, must be men of character, integrity, capacity and judicial temperament.

"The tendency of some men to become tyrants" upon mounting the bench is well known and most unfortunate, he adds. "If a judge becomes a tyrant when he is young, he's likely to remain a tyrant".

Hence, Godwin sought to exercise extra care with his selections or nominations.

The record would seem to suggest that he did an exceptional job.

Looking through Capitol's columns at history: Part of the half-frozen crowd which attended the Godwin inaugural.

FIRST LADY: LIFE IN THE MANSION

"The Governor's Mansion is possessed of a sense of history and you can't get away from it. Yet, it is a beautiful old home that is very liveable, even in its isolation in Capitol Square. It requires cautious care to protect it from wear and tear".

So says Katherine Godwin of the lovely old building in which the Commonwealth of Virginia has housed its governors and their families since 1813. It's real name is "Executive Mansion" and there is a bronze plaque by the front door to remind every occupant of the illustrious company he keeps.

Famous personages from Lafayette to Churchill have been guests and one bedroom is named for the Frenchman who helped America win its independence. His visit was in 1824. Here was brought the body of Stonewall Jackson in 1863 after he was accidentally fatally wounded by his own men.

Within its friendly walls there has been only one wedding but, like any reputable old Virginia ante-bellum home, it boasts a ghost said to be that of a pretty young lady in rustling taffeta, ready for the grand ball.

When it was erected on a knoll near the Capitol on orders of the General Assembly, it looked out over the James River and governors could see sailing ships tied up at docks below the rapids. Now, high office buildings surround it and obscure the view and there are no other homes anywhere near.

Nevertheless, the beautiful two-story brick mansion designed by Alexander Parris of Boston and modified by the Assembly's commission, has continued Virginia's pride and joy. An oval dining room was added in 1906, an adjoining breakfast room with library above being constructed during the tenure of Gov. and Mrs. J. Lindsay Almond, Jr. in 1958.

Over the 157 years of its existence it has gone from fireplace heating to central heat and air conditioning and even has a small concealed elevator. Governor W. M. Tuck modernized its bathrooms, adding tubs big enough for a big man.

Now that the former kitchen and employe quarters (a sep-

Virginia's First Lady: Katherine Godwin looks to the silver and place settings for a dinner in the Mansion.

arate building) has been converted into a guest house, the Mansion's ample half-basement contains kitchen, pantry, laundry, baths and staff quarters as well as place for a Capitol policeman who stands guard at night from the inside.

Like the White House, the Mansion's first floor rooms are "public rooms" although infrequently these days, while the second floor or "apartment" is strictly private. Only a few close friends ever see its hallway sitting room or the library-television room, most popular and most lived-in of all. All furniture is state-owned.

Each governor and first lady leave something of themselves behind after their four years and the Godwins will be no exception. Incidentally, Gov. and Mrs. Albertis S. Harrison, Jr. had a beautiful 20-page full color booklet on the Mansion published and sent to fortunate friends at Christmas 1965.

Katherine Godwin had been a frequent guest here before she came through the door as its mistress for four years on January 15, 1966. She didn't regard it as a public museum exactly but, on the other hand, she realized that it was going to be a far cry from the comfortable home in Chuckatuck.

Just as she had never dreamed of his entering politics when they were married, so was she sure that he had never dreamed of being Governor of Virginia after his first election to the House of Delegates in 1947. But here they were and with an excited little girl of 12 to help make it a home.

The problems began the first day they moved in. The first big snow of inaugural night was followed by others and within a week clogged gutters had caused leaks in upstairs rooms and hall. That called for quick repairs, then new painting and wall paper.

Later Mrs. Godwin was to select some new carpet both upstairs and down, acquire some new furniture, have other furniture re-upholstered, re-paper the breakfast room and re-do dining room chairs.

Especially is she proud of two dining end chairs with crewel work state seals on the backs made in England. The new carpet of the ballroom and matching white and gold drapes are elegant.

At the same time, the guest house has had new paint, wall paper, curtains and some furniture.

"My main purpose was not to come in and make changes. I tried to hold to the old, improve it and provide a better look. The ball room rugs had worn out and with the new ones it is no longer depressing".

It was a good thing for her that they had been accustomed to early rising in Chuckatuck so that Mills could have a leisurely breakfast then drive the 10 miles to Suffolk to his law office to be ready for work there or for opening of court.

"I have had to get up by six-thirty or I couldn't make it", she says with a sparkle in her eye. For the first three years, at least, she customarily had fruit and coffee with Becky and then got her off to school before finishing breakfast with the Governor.

"The wife is the one who should adjust" is her philosophy. "He must be happy in his work. He must have the right to make his choice of occupation for that is the big thing in his life". This much she decided when he entered politics.

Fortunately for the Governor's wife, he never got in the habit of bringing his office work home to the Mansion. He tried to clear his desk before leaving.

"He has needed a change of atmosphere and a different environment at home", she says. No, she never had to call him to come to dinner.

"He always knows what time it is", she laughs.

In return, Katherine Godwin bothered her husband in his office as little as possible.

"I don't suppose I've been over there a dozen times in four years", she adds.

Among the many social functions they were to give in the next four years several have special memories.

There were, for example, dinners for their families and close friends and one for U. S. Chief Justice and Mrs. Warren Burger.

Then, there was the dinner in October, 1966, for those ministers and wives who had been close friends of all three Godwins going back to his boyhood. None had ever been in the Mansion before.

Then there was the reception in the spring of 1967 for 500 people from Chuckatuck—just about everybody from in or near the town—again a first for most of the guests who came by bus and private automobile and had a wonderful time. Star of the evening was hometowner Charlie Byrd, a concert guitarist, and his vocalist wife, who with others in his band had made a big name at the White House.

There were, of course, the usual dinners in honor of State Supreme Court justices and their wives and at various times for members of the General Assembly and their wives, distinguished visitors from around the Nation and from abroad.

During Christmas holidays of 1967 there was a black tie affair for 250 friends from Suffolk, another memorable occasion. In 1969 there was a dinner for their doctor friends and particularly medical men who waged Becky's last valiant fight.

Getting Ready for Christmas. The 150-year-old Governor's Mansion lends itself to gracious holiday atmosphere. Here Tom Bannister, the veteran head butler of more than 40 years, helps Mrs. Godwin decorate the 1966 tree in archway to the ballroom.

On their final Sunday in the Mansion the Godwins would play host to the pastor and entire congregation of St. John's United Church of Christ—their "church away from home".

Being the First Lady proved to be no easy matter for it involved running the Mansion, being hostess for countless events, directing the staff of seven in their daily work and finding time to make public appearances or travelling with the Governor around the state.

The staff went with the Mansion. Veteran of them all is Tom Bannister, the butler known to most regular visitors, who came in 1926 with Governor Byrd as a chauffeur; Lucille Anderson, who was brought in as cook by Governor Price and probably has tickled more appetites than anyone ever associated with the Mansion; and Raymond Wilson, butler and general handyman who came with the Godwins.

Then there are the three maids—Alease Elam, Beatrice Bailey and Pearl Hockaday. Alease, who came with the Almonds, is upstairs maid, tending to the linens, making the beds and seeing that the living quarters are spotless. Bernice Williams, who came with the Stanleys, runs the laundry.

Until the Godwins' arrival, heavy cleaning as well as yard work was done by "trusty" prisoners from the State Penitentiary.

The Governor's wife talks with each staff member daily, plans the meals with Lucille and sometimes serves as peacemaker when inter-departmental difficulties arise.

Mrs. Godwin thinks there should be two more employes—a private secretary for the Governor's wife and a housekeeper. Governor Tuck had a housekeeper and she feels the State should provide one from now on. As far as a secretary is concerned, when mail has become too heavy, she has had to ask assistance at the Governor's office.

One thing she learned early: while the State may own the liquor monopoly it doesn't furnish a supply to the Mansion. Drinks are on the Governor and this can be a not inconsiderable item.

An unwritten rule is that there must be flower arrangements in the public rooms, especially the entrance hall and the dining room, and often in the ballroom, sitting room and drawing room.

This is a big task and fortunately for Katherine Godwin she has had the expert volunteer services of two good friends.

Polly Brooks, wife of A. Gordon Brooks, director of the Division of Teacher Training in the State Department of Education, who lived across the street from the Godwins in Chuckatuck when they were both young married couples, was the chief arranger who spent many hours in the Mansion daily. In fact, since the tragic events of August, 1968, the Brooks practically lived there.

Assisting her has been Mrs. Herbert Carl Lee, wife of a surgeon at the Medical College of Virginia. Once, when the Speaker of the British House of Commons was a distinguished guest and wanted magnolias and mint juleps, Mrs. Brooks provided the magnolias and Mrs. Lee managed the juleps Virginia style.

Frequently, the Governor brought visitors to lunch for a bit of Old Dominion hospitality and perhaps a "soft sell". Usually, however, he came alone for a quick lunch and a half hour of relaxation.

The dinner hour was always private for the family unless there were a few close friends or guests. Two or three times a week there seemed to be dinners or banquets but they disliked "having a big show every night". Traveling about the state as well as to national conferences and even abroad kept them away more than they would have liked.

"Living in a goldfish bowl" like the Mansion brought necessity to get away from it all and frequently they went to Colonial Williamsburg which all three loved and stayed at the Allen-Byrd House, the Inn or the Lodge.

It became necessary to turn down far more invitations than they could accept to homes and to organization functions because this could get out of hand and prevent them having any private lives at all.

One thing Katherine Godwin never would do and that was make the speech circuit. On very rare occasion she told a woman's group about Mansion history or life there but while she likes people she has a deep aversion to crusading.

"Every action", she says, "is observed by people. The Governor's wife has to be more careful of her person. Women

70

First Family at Home: In Governor's Library on the first floor of the Mansion, Mrs. Godwin and teenager Becky catch the man of the house for a bit of small talk.

notice clothes. The Governor's wife is pointed out wherever she goes. There is always a question of what to wear. Whatever you do or say must be done cautiously. I just try to be natural—I could not pretend".

Katherine Godwin was destined to have more than her share of trouble and tragedy while a resident in the Mansion.

On July 2, 1967, she suffered a broken ankle in an automobile accident near Waynesboro when another car pulled from a side road into the path of the Governor's limousine. The mother of the other driver was killed. That cost several weeks in the University of Virginia Hospital and six months recuperating. Again while Mrs. Godwin was recovering from surgery in August, 1968, Becky died tragically.

Thus, the First Lady's last year and a half in the Mansion was to be lived under circumstances which would have tested the courage, faith and heart of any woman. She was to be glad when January 17, 1970 arrived.

Throughout her four years in this great old home she was always conscious of those who had lived there before.

Did any of them return? Only Mrs. John Garland Pollard, Mrs. J. Lindsay Almond, Jr. and Mrs. Albertis S. Harrison, Jr., all of whom were happy to see their innovations preserved.

Mercifully, the good only is remembered and the bad forgotten. Each knew in part what she experienced. They were sisters in an elite sorority.

Undoubtedly the most excited member of the Godwin family on the cold winter day it moved into the Mansion was 12-year-old Becky—pretty, brown haired, brown eyed and dimpled with a charming smile and unaffected manner which made her at once the darling of Capitol Square.

She was the first child to live in the Mansion in many years and would be the first teenager to call it home since the days of Governor and Mrs. Colgate W. Darden, Jr. during World War II.

One of the great regrets of Katherine and Mills Godwin had been that they were denied the joy of children they both loved—he from a big family and she a school teacher. Thus it was that they planned to adopt a child.

Arrangements for that happy event were made in September, 1953, and in January 1954 a tiny infant came to live in the pleasant two-story brick house in Chuckatuck. As babies have a habit of doing, she completely changed the routine of the Godwins but never was a child more loved or welcome.

Babyhood and childhood for Becky—that was her only name until she gave herself another—were normal for a little country town with a big yard to grow up in. There were all sorts of chances to be spoiled by indulgent neighbors such as the Henry Grady Norfleets next door but she didn't spoil easily.

At six she had started to school in the same building where her Mother had taught over a decade before and she made many little friends, the closest being Kathy Saunders.

Soon she had a kitten which she named "Muff" but in 1961 a problem arose. She had been wanting a puppy and knowing this, the Nansemond game warden, Joby Jones, gave her a Manchester terrier, then a year old. Unfortunately, the terrier named "Ginny", didn't get on well with the cat and so "Muff" went next door to live with the Norfleets.

Fond of the outdoors like her father, Becky soon had a pony she dubbed "Sweetheart" and which lived not far away on the

72

family farm at Holladay's Point. There she and her friends often enjoyed riding in the fields.

Mills Godwin already had been in the Senate two years when Becky arrived and he had always been in public life so far as she knew. Except for brief visits to Richmond, she and her Mother stayed in Chuckatuck when the General Assembly was in session. But on those visits—a Senate baby being a rarity—she was the center of attention.

Mutual Admiration Society: Daddy was just home from the hospital in December, 1955, and little Becky was delighted to tell him of her happiness.

The first time she showed any interest in her Daddy's campaigns was when he was running for lieutenant governor and then it was to ask what would happen to "Mr. Gi Stephens sitting up there in that big chair". The thought of Godwin losing never entered her mind.

The big excitement was to come four years later on the night of Nov. 2, 1965. After listening to election returns at home in Chuckatuck, they drove into Richmond and as they passed the main gate of Capitol Square opposite Hotel Richmond, Godwin pointed to the Mansion behind the capitol and said:

"Becky, this will be your home for the next four years".

She hardly could believe it—a house among all those great tall buildings—but the excitement grew as arrangements were made to enter her in the well-known St. Catherine's School and the time for the inauguration came closer. Not even a week's trip to Fort Lauderdale, Florida, Godwin's favorite vacation spot, and the Christmas holidays could dull the excitement. They made the trip by train because Becky did not like to fly.

The inauguration with all its glamour failed to impress the little girl unless it was the parade which followed and even then the numbing cold failed to make that much of an attraction. Besides, she didn't like being in the public eye and was anxious to explore that big house.

On Way to the Inaugural: The Godwin family smile their happiness as does incoming Lt. Gov. Fred G. Pollard (behind Mrs. Godwin). P.S.— The Governor wore Long Johns for the occasion.

The enthusiasm of the Mansion staff and the Capitol Police, who guard the Governor's family and the Capitol grounds, at having a child around knew no bounds. Thus it was that well before the new Governor and First Lady could get settled Becky had learned all details of the telephone system, the intercom system, the elevator which runs from basement to second floor and—best of all to an impressionable little girl—the fascinating tunnels which connect the Mansion with the Capitol and other State buildings, housing the water, electric and heating systems besides affording safe passage in the worst weather.

Becky loved her own private bedroom with bath and quickly learned details about the beautiful old Mansion—the private suites of the Governor and First Lady, the upstairs sitting room which is really the hallway, the library or den where the television has been situated, and the more formal rooms of the first floor as well as the labyrinth of the basement—what fun to explore!

Then, there was the guest house, built as the Mansion kitchen and used for a variety of purposes over the years, which had been so beautifully remodelled and furnished in the Stanley and Almond regimes. It was here that Becky gave her first big Christmas party in 1967 for 18 girls from St. Catherine's with a heavy snow adding to the fun. The restored garden, so private and secluded behind its high brick walls, was also a delight.

But life in the Governor's Mansion can be lonely for a child and not what it was a century or even a half century ago. There are no other residences or schools for many, many blocks distance. It is absolutely isolated, a fact which few realize.

As a result, Becky had to be driven to St. Catherine's School, usually by a Capitol Policeman who picked her up again in the afternoon. She didn't like that and rebelled for a while. She didn't want to be seen in the big limousine with the No. 1 State license plate, preferring the station wagon or the "second car" without markings.

Even then, the shy child disliked being the object of curiosity from Capitol visitors. One officer recalls with a chuckle that she would crouch down out of sight until they cleared Capitol Square.

The busy parents worried about her adjustment but with typical independence she made out. Headmaster Robert W.

Trusdell and her teachers took a special interest in her. Her grades were good, she became an omnivorous reader.

Playmates were something else, however. Either classmates from St. Catherine's had to be brought for visits or she went to their homes, especially loving those in the suburbs where there were horses to be ridden. Occasionally they went to the movies or to the Jewish Recreation Center.

Around the Capitol, the police loved to spoil her. They put up a basketball hoop on the wall behind the garden and there they shot baskets with her. Once in a while her Daddy, who had been a pretty fair player in his time, stopped to play. They idolized one another.

C. J. Marion of the Capitol Police recalls how he helped her with a botany project at school. They catalogued every variety of tree on the Capitol grounds including magnolia, elm, oak, sycamore and maple. She learned to identify each one by its leaves and reported a good grade for her efforts.

"We all loved that child", he says.

It was not uncommon to see a girl bicycling or skating around the square accompanied by an officer. She also learned to ice skate and had a sled for the Capitol hill when there was snow. A rare treat came when her bosom pal, Kathy Saunders, came from Chuckatuck for a visit.

There was always a close mother-daughter relationship and they talked of many things that concern a girl growing up. There was the glow that only a mother can know when Becky came home one day and announced that she had decided that she wanted a middle name and that it would be Katherine.

There was more feeling of satisfaction when she commented: "I know that I'm adopted but that doesn't make any difference". It didn't unless it was that they loved her more.

"She made a good adjustment when she found this big thing descending on her", recalls Mrs. Godwin. "She liked to look at her Daddy's progress from a distance and not to be in the public eye herself. She thought the girls at St. Catherine's might like her because she was the Governor's daughter. So I was pleased one day when she came home from school and said: 'I'm convinced my friends are my friends because I'm me' ".

76

Much of summers in 1966, 1967 and 1968 were spent at Camp Sequoya, operated by Sullins College between Bristol and Abingdon with Mrs. Raymond Bailey in charge. She learned to water ski, passed her junior life saving test and loved all sports.

As mischevious as any other child, Becky loved jokes and pranks. As a matter of fact, she brought on her father's first law and order problem a few days after inauguration. It had snowed heavily, as it did most of January, and there was a telephoned instruction from the Governor's office to the Mansion that Becky and Scotty Ginn, granddaughter of Attorney General Button, cease and desist from snowballing passersby along Governor Street on the backside of Capitol Square.

Late that year, shortly before Thanksgiving, the Mattaponi Indians came up from their reservation to present the Governor with their annual tribute of game, usually a deer and turkey.

Chief Custalow spotted the little girl shyly watching from the background and invited her to join him in an Indian dance which she did, much to the delight of most of Virginia because the television crews were there to record it all.

In time Becky discovered she had to wear glasses which she didn't mind too much but as she became more the young lady contact lenses were welcome. She enjoyed the Cotillion Club where she learned to dance well under tutelage of Miss Cleiland Donnan as well as the need for poise.

There were parties and pajama affairs but no dating with boys for Mrs. Godwin is not one of those who believe in rushing children into adulthood.

There were, of course, occasional weekend trips back to the home in Chuckatuck where she could see friends and go to Sunday School at Oakland Church. Most Sundays found them at St. John's United Church of Christ in Richmond, their church-away-from-home, where the Rev. Richard Cheek, pastor, had two daughters and a son near Becky's age.

Two widely separated events helped overcome her fear of flying. Once, in Cairo, the Godwins discovered that the only way they could get to Israel and the Holy Land sites which Becky had her heart set on seeing, was to fly—by devious route, of course, since direct Arab-Israeli connections are impossible.

Informed of this, she reluctantly consented and they flew

into Lod Airport, midway between Jerusalem and Tel Aviv, much to her relief.

The other time was when the Governor was going to pay an official visit to Expo-67 in Montreal. Sufficient time for train travel, her favorite, was lacking and so, after considering the invitation to accompany her father, she agreed. They had a great time at the World Fair.

As an avid fisherman, Godwin taught Becky to fish as he would have taught a son. Especially did she enjoy their excursions on the Nansemond, the James, Hampton Roads and Chesapeake Bay.

The Commission of Fisheries boat "Chesapeake" serves as the unofficial gubernatorial yacht and she loved travel in this manner.

Often, too, Governor and daughter were buddies at baseball games of the Richmond Virginians in the International League. In the Governor's box they ate popcorn and hot dogs with relish while rooting for the home team.

Becky was, in Mrs. Godwin's words, "truly at heart a little girl—full of fun, mischief and jokes".

She made the great gray Mansion a home.

Off to School: Mother gets in a final word to bubbling, brown-eyed Becky as she leaves the mansion with armful of books. George Washington statue in background seems pointing the way.
—Richmond Newspapers Photo

THE SALES TAX: KEY TO PROGRESS

On November 10, 1965, Governor-elect Mills Godwin was vacationing with Mrs. Godwin and daughter Becky in Fort Lauderdale, Florida, seeking to rest after the rigors of his successful campaign, when a telephone call came from Harry F. Byrd, Jr.

The younger Byrd said that his father had transmitted a letter of resignation from the U. S. Senate to Governor Harrison and he was interested in appointment to the unexpired term.

Having been aware of the older man's illness, Godwin was not exactly surprised although the timing of the announcement caught him slightly unprepared.

Remembering his long friendship with both father and son and especially how Harry, Jr. had stood aside to clear the way for his nomination without contest, Godwin gladly gave his backing and called Governor Harrison later in the day.

As a matter of fact, he was glad to have Harrison make the appointment for a number of reasons. They both knew that the sales tax issue was coming up at the 1966 legislative session, now only days away, and that both Byrds had opposed it in the past.

Harrison announced the resignation November 11 and the appointment of young Byrd the next day. There was criticism, of course, especially over the speed of action and nothing favorable could be expected from foes of the Byrds.

Harry, Jr. took his seat almost at once and became, in Godwin's opinion "a very good member of the Senate who has served Virginia and the country with great distinction".

Both men were happy, Byrd having achieved an ambition and Godwin pleased that Byrd's considerable influence in the State Senate and House alike had been removed so that he would not be in conflict with the program Godwin envisaged.

There was little possibility that the senior Senator, in retirement which lasted only a year until his death, would stand in the way. Actually, he had withdrawn his interest in state politics as early as 1960 and visiting Washington in January 1965, Godwin found him far more interested in talking about what had happened 40 years before.

Undoubtedly, Byrd Senior realized that times were changing in his state. Many in his Organization were aware as the 1960's opened that the state was falling behind in its support of schools, colleges, hospitals, highways and other governmental responsibilities.

In addition, with the influx of new industry bringing thousands of new people and with levels of leadership in management not oriented toward Virginia conservatism, Byrd and his followers were beginning to feel the weight of criticism.

Thus it was that Godwin was not the only Organization stalwart who found the aging Senator becoming gradually aloof and apart from things on the state level.

"Senator Byrd had been a dominant figure for 40 years", says Godwin. "I had been a supporter of his for many years, as had my father and the whole Godwin family. But times had to change. His era ended perhaps with his retirement, maybe even before, and a new era was evolving—what shape it will take none can say for sure even now".

Another sign of the times was that Byrd's neighbor and long-time political associate, Speaker E. Blackburn (Blackie) Moore also would retire in another two years. A close friend of the new Governor, he nevertheless stuck to pay-as-you-go and never supported the sales tax at any point.

There was no question in Godwin's mind that he now would be the unquestioned leader of his party as well as his state. Keenly aware that political squabbling had denied him a majority, he nevertheless resolved that he was going to be the Governor of all Virginia in spirit as well as in fact.

Known until the recent campaign as an arch-conservative, a massive resistance leader and as a representative of the Southside, rural brand of thinking, he had displayed as a candidate remarkable shifting in basic philosophy. In so doing, he had made promises, painted pictures and shared dreams that now must be fulfilled or he would see his career blighted and his party fragmented beyond recovery.

Fortunately for him, the thinking of the people had been changing and he was quick to recognize it. In addition, the character of the General Assembly had been altered substantially, although not radically, by the 1964 reapportionment which followed the U. S. Supreme Court's one man-one vote decision. This helped to end rural domination which had existed since the first House of Burgesses met at Jamestown in 1619. It gave greater power to the urban areas, especially around Hampton Roads.

That fact in turn was to prove decisive in the historic struggle over a retail sales tax, the key to Godwin's whole plan of progress for Virginia.

Mills Godwin had attended and suffered through the spine-tingling cold of a good many other inaugurations with long speeches which benumbed crowds sat through but failed to hear, waiting later to get details from the newspapers. Consequently, he resolved to keep his short and provide details in an address to a joint session of the General Assembly.

At the Microphone

The 11-minute inaugural with its emphasis on education and its key phrase: "knowledge is the great equalizer of our time", was appreciated and drew prompt and generous response from a people who understood what he meant. Modestly, he admits it probably was one of his better speeches.

The inaugural and its accompanying festivities behind him, the new Governor had until Monday noon to get his breath before delivering a carefully prepared message to the Assembly. The weight of reality descended.

"With all the pomp and circumstance of an inaugural, one is a little numb, finding it hard to believe it is happening to him", he recalls four years later. "But it doesn't take him long to realize that the realities of the situation are at hand and it was impressed upon me pretty quickly.

"The heavy responsibility that falls on your shoulders as you take the oath is not something to be treated lightly. I don't know anything that happens to any man any time that is more sobering. People were anxious to see the state get moving and so I was face to face with the situation on Monday morning".

The message he was about to deliver contained the blueprint of his program, destined to bring on one of the most influential legislative showdowns of the century. A master politician was needed at the helm and, as events were to prove, Mills Godwin had what it took.

As previously noted, 15 cities had enacted sales taxes by the time the 1966 General Assembly convened. Shortly before, the Virginia Advisory Legislative Council, an invaluable study group made up of legislators from both houses and with access to the state's best brains outside of government, had handed in a report urging that the state take over the entire cost of paying teachers. It proposed to finance this with a 3 per cent retail sales tax, collected by the state, with one-third going to the localities. Opposition quickly developed.

Outgoing Governor Harrison and incoming Governor Godwin were in agreement on many things, undoubtedly the biggest one being the necessity for a sales tax. They differed only on some details, such as distribution.

These two had come to the General Assembly on the same day in 1948, Harrison to the Senate, Godwin to the House. They had been acquainted previously through legal circles and the work of Commonwealth attorney offices. They had become fast friends with a respect that ripened in the Senate. When Harrison moved up from attorney general to the governorship, Godwin rose to lieutenant governor. Harrison had encouraged Godwin's ambition to the Mansion, had sponsored him in the campaign and recently had done everything possible to smooth the way in the transition between administrations.

On January 12, in almost his last act as governor, Harrison

had eased the way for his successor by proposing a 3 per cent retail sales tax—2 per cent to be effective September 1 and the other 1 per cent on July 1, 1968. He proposed in the same breath that local sales taxes be abolished as a "spreading patchwork pattern" with harmful implications for state.

This was to help finance a $2.2 billion budget for the 1966-68 biennium and was $600 million above the budget then in force. It also contained $100 million for capital improvements, anticipating a $96 million surplus by June 30. It also left Godwin $15 million "to play with", as the legislative expression has it.

The burden of Harrison's plea was that the Assembly act promptly to keep the cities from preempting the state's "last major new source of revenue". While advocating a sales tax, he did not have a bill introduced.

If anyone doubts how swiftly changes can come in state policy and in the minds of governors and legislators, be it remembered here that only six years before Gov. J. Lindsay Almond, Jr. had advocated a 3 per cent retail sales tax. Two influential men who helped kill it in the Senate Finance Committee were Mills Godwin and Harry Byrd, Jr.

(It should be noted here that the two sales tax plans were substantially different—so much so that "Sales Tax Sam" Pope had refused to patron the Almond proposal.)

Now things were different and just before Governor Godwin spoke, the situation was dramatized by jovial, freckle-faced, red-haired Pope, of Southhampton County, who had offered sales tax measures for years without success.

Amid the usual laughter and cheers, Sam put his latest version in the hopper—not too far from what Godwin wanted but containing provision for a $60 income tax cut. That idea never had a chance

In his pilot message, Godwin asked, like Harrison for 2 per cent September 1 and another one per cent July 1, 1968. He suggested that the first penny go to localities, based on school population rather than the formula suggested by Harrison.

"The question before us is not *whether* to adopt a general retail sales tax but *how* it shall be imposed and more specifically how the proceeds shall be *distributed*", he told the legislators.

Four years later he recalls: "I believed that the money

should go where the children were. But I would be less than candid if I did not say now that there were some political reasons for the suggestions".

He realized that under his plan more localities, especially counties, would benefit, that urban areas such as the Hampton Roads cities would fare well although a few such as Richmond and Northern Virginia might be hurt at first. They wanted the tax distribution based on sales and this would penalize rural areas.

Godwin did not say whether the localities should have the right to levy an additional one per cent tax. He felt that this would not be overlooked and events quickly proved him correct.

"Your only true guide", he told the legislators, "is to put above all else what is right, what is fair, what is equitable, what will meet the present and future needs of Virginia—not part of Virginia, but all of Virginia".

Because the Godwin version still had to be written by bill drafters it wasn't "sent downstairs" until January 28. It allowed localities to levy an extra one per cent and gave one half of the state's share to cities and counties based on school age population. A companion bill carried a 2 per cent excise or titling tax on automobiles.

The remainder of the program he submitted in his first message centered on seven points: $700 million increase in teacher salaries, rejecting the VALC recommendation that the state bear the whole load; creation of a system of 22 Community Colleges with a single board in charge; merger of Richmond Professional Institute and the Medical College of Virginia into Virginia Commonwealth University and making George Mason and Christopher Newport two-year colleges four-year institutions; 100 additional state troopers; increased appropriation to start a 10-year program urged by the Virginia Outdoor and Recreation Study Commission; a commission to study metropolitan problems; an increase in workmen's unemployment compensation and better staffing at mental hospitals.

The sales tax—a break with the tradition of 123 years— was the key and focal point which deserves special treatment for the political maneuvering and polite persuasion which finally brought it to reality, as we shall see next.

84

PUTTING OVER THE SALES TAX:
A LESSON IN PRACTICAL POLITICS

Putting the Pen to History: Governor Godwin signs the sales tax bill with chief patrons Sen. Edward L. Breeden of Norfolk and Del. Samuel E. (Sales Tax Sam) Pope in happy mood, March 1966.

Few people ever hear about the maneuvering which takes place behind the scenes in bringing about the passage or defeat of a piece of legislation—the backing and filling, the horse trading, the political arm-twisting and the downright pleading for votes, sometimes accompanied by the dangling of political plums.

Because the retail sales tax approved by the General Assembly in 1966 was the first new broad-based tax increase since

1843 (there had been an income tax law on the books since 1848) it should be interesting to have on the record Governor Godwin's own account of what happened and how it happened.

The Governor had just returned to his office from lunch after delivery of his special message to the joint session on January 17 when a secretary informed him that Sen. Edward L. Breeden of Norfolk and a large delegation from Tidewater communities were waiting.

"This, I hoped, was the break I had been almost praying for and it was", he recalls.

Acting as spokesman, Breeden said that they would like to support the Godwin sales tax program and could go along with everything he had suggested in his message if he could make one concession. Their cities already had a sales tax (2 per cent in nearly all cases) and must have it to make fiscal ends meet.

They had noted, Breeden observed, that Godwin had omitted mention of a local tax to be imposed above the state levy. They asked that the Governor accept the idea of making a local tax optional and in addition that the state assume all costs of collection and distribution.

Godwin promised to study the matter and give them an early answer because he felt that immediate action was imperative.

"I wanted the one per cent escalation clause written in. Mr. Morrissett (Tax Commissioner C. H. Morrissett), Mr. Day (State Comptroller Sidney C. Day) and Mr. Kuhn (Budget Director L. M. Kuhn) were urging it and it was apparent that we would have to have the money in 1968. This additional penny would be preserved to the state".

Two days later, on Wednesday, the Governor called back the Tidewater group and told them that he would recommend their request for local option if they would support him on the escalation clause and other revenue measures he proposed.

"I felt that success was near", he recollects. "Richmond and a few other localities were the main foes but we were well on the way to winning one of the great battles".

Senator Breeden, a member of the General Assembly since 1936 and a Senator since 1944, now became close advisor and floor leader for most of the Godwin program.

"It would be impossible to express adequately appreciation

to him for his work in piloting the tax legislation through its stormy course", admits the Governor.

Godwin now turned to Morrissett to draft the sales tax bill. The Tax Commissioner never advocated this levy but went along as a loyal official, implicitly trusted by so many governors.

"He asked if I would give him a few days to work on it and to consult the attorney general (Robert Y. Button). This I agreed to and he took his yellow legal pad and went home.

"I didn't see him again for five days until he came back with the rough draft, written out in long hand and containing all the provisions that he and I felt were desirable and necessary".

The Morrissett draft permitted local option of one per cent additional tax based on the point of sale and this, recalls Godwin, "had a levelling influence against opponents of the school age distribution formula. It also contained the escalation clause. This was an unprecedented proposal not only for Virginia but for the nation. No other state had ever tried to impose a tax increase over two years in advance".

"I realized the political difficulties involved", he says, "and so I mustered my arguments. Mr. Morrissett was a strong advocate. We were afraid of what would happen if the additional one per cent was left to 1968. It is not likely we could have gotten by without it—it was not, however, an easy thing to sell to the General Assembly".

Finally the typing and polishing was done and the companion bills were ready for House and Senate introduction just 11 days after the Governor had delivered his outline to the Assembly.

Amid more cheers and applause, Sam Pope dropped the House version in the hopper and it promptly went to the Finance Committee where Del. John Warren Cooke of Matthews was acting chairman most of the time in the illness-caused absence of Chairman Charles K. Hutchens of Newport News. Cooke was co-patron of the House bill and as Floor Leader had great influence.

Senators Breeden and J. D. Hagood, the veteran from Clover, served as co-patrons of the Senate counterpart.

Reported to the House floor intact, the bill now was subject of lively and prolonged debate, a critical point coming when an amendment was offered to eliminate the escalation clause. Here the Governor suffered his first defeat. The amendment carried, 45 to 44.

What happened to the other eleven of the 100-member House? Why would so many miss a vital roll call? Recalls Godwin:

"Several members who we had counted against the amendment went out conveniently to get a drink of water or a cup of coffee just as the vote was about to be taken".

It was obvious that they were not anxious to be recorded on such a controversial issue.

One member later told the Governor that he voted for the amendment when he meant to vote against—throwing his switch to green instead of red. Had he voted as he intended there would have been a tie and the amendment would have lost.

Speaker E. Blackburn Moore voted aye and Godwin felt that he had helped carry the day.

The Tidewater delegation kept their word and many of the Organization stalwarts also stood with the Administration.

Republicans, except for Russell Davis of Franklin County, supported the amendment and opposed the bill, something which reminds Godwin of an incident which happened at Williamsburg in 1968. CBS-Tv Newsman Walter Cronkite asked the Governor how many Republicans were in the General Assembly.

"Nineteen", Godwin replied, only to be corrected by a Republican nearby who made it 20.

"But you count Russell Davis", joked the Governor, "and I don't because he votes Democratic most of the time!"

The question now was whether the escalator clause should be forgotten or an effort made at reconsideration.

"My advisors were mixed in their feelings so I decided why gamble?—not to ask for reconsideration. It was not good politics. I felt it best to try to get the bill with the escalator through the Senate then bring it back to the House for concurrence".

Godwin made his wishes clear at a press conference on Friday and after a private poll discovered he had 11 votes in the

Senate Finance Committee. By a 12 to 7 vote the committee restored the escalator clause to the House measure. Now the task was to muster 21 votes on the Senate floor.

Both his opponents there and a good portion of the state press took the line that the tax increase could wait until 1968.

"But", says Godwin, "I could see the lines hardening—I pleaded, I argued and I prayed. I had Judge Morrissett go before the Finance Committee and explain just how badly we would need the money. He told them that in his opinion it would be foolhardy to pass the bill without this provision in it. This helped fortify my position immensely".

The Senate accepted the escalator 24 to 16 with Republicans furnishing much of the opposition and passed the bill overwhelmingly.

The question now was: what will the House do on Monday?

Let the Governor tell it:

"That weekend I stayed on the telephone at the Mansion or in my office—Friday night, Saturday, Saturday night, all day Sunday and even Sunday night trying to see that the votes would be available when needed. Never have I been as intensely interested nor have I been as persuasive as I attempted to be in this issue. I not only talked to members at home—I called many of the friends of those in doubt and tried to get them to help us.

"The first break came in connection with the two delegates from the City of Hampton, Messrs. Bagley (Richard Marshall) and Gray (John David). They had voted for the amendment. The Senator from Hampton, Hunter Andrews, had voted to put the one per cent back in the bill in the Senate.

"I thought this was a good place to start. I asked my good friend Mr. Andrews to call Messrs. Bagley and Gray. I talked to them myself several times. They were not particularly hostile but were unwilling to commit themselves.

"I called my good friend, Congressman Tom Downing, who was likewise their good friend and asked him to talk to them. I also called Sidney Kellam (at Virginia Beach) who had a very close relationship with the Hampton group at that time and asked him to help. Both of them did.

"Tom called me at home Sunday night and said I would have the votes of Bagley and Gray to sustain the Senate bill.

Ironing Out the Sales Tax Kinks: Gov. Godwin confers with legislative leaders in an effort to reach agreement. From left, Sen. Edward L. Breeden, of Norfolk; Del. George H. Hill, of Newport News; Sen. William B. Spong, Jr., of Portsmouth and Sen. William H. Hodges of Chesapeake.

"This was one of the first tangible evidences I had of switches of votes.

"Early Monday morning when I got to the office I could see the tide was beginning to turn. T. Coleman Andrews, Jr., of Richmond, was one of the first to come in and say that he would support the Senate amendment. Then came Edward E. Lane and others of the Richmond delegation. We were over the hump. The House reconsidered and accepted the amendment by 66 to 33.

"We had a great bill—a model for other states. I was proud of the victory. I have not received as much satisfaction on any legislative action as I did on this particular bill".

He had, indeed, pulled it through the critical stage almost single-handed, demonstrating not only tremendous powers of persuasion but uncommon political know-how and indomitable will in the clutch. He had headed off a rugged battle two years hence in the 1968 General Assembly and guaranteed the funds so necessary to full realization of his program, especially for public schools and higher education.

How did he feel in the wake of that triumph?

"The bill had to be zealously guarded. Several legislators were asking for what were really minor amendments that in themselves were not harmful but I had to refuse because I was

90

afraid of the consequences if it got back on the floor of the Assembly. I signed the bill as soon as it was enrolled.

"The story of the legislation is fascinating and culminated a long effort to expand the tax base. We talked then of $50 million per penny from the tax and it is now $70 million.

"This has done so much good in the localities and in the state that it is difficult to assess its true significance.

"I, of course, will be remembered as the Governor who put the sales tax on and it is not a popular thing in some quarters as to certain features, but there has been a very small volume of mail in my office that has objected. There has been some resentment, mostly generated as pertaining to food and non-prescription drugs but even there it has been limited to political candidates in the heat of a campaign.

"Forty-six states now have the sales tax and 31 tax food and non-prescription drugs. Benefits flow from it that are very great. To take the tax off food would reduce the revenue 25 per cent and if we take it off non-prescription drugs, there would be another reduction of 3 per cent.

"This 28 per cent cut would apply to the local as well as the state tax and the localities would suffer".

He admits the tax is not perfect but is proud of the manner in which it has been set up and administered. It has, he believes, gotten Virginia off to a good start on the high road of progress on all levels, especially education.

Godwin was prepared for a flood of adversely critical mail but was surprised when it did not materialize.

Amused, he recalls that there was far greater furore in May 1966 over "Pokey", the whale which strayed up the James as far as Hopewell, fought off all efforts to tow him to sea, was "whale-tied" and shot by an ambitious farmer and eventually died.

But after the sales tax went into effect September 1 there was considerable wry joke-making about it.

At mid-month, Gov. Godwin was at Hotel Roanoke to make one of his countless addresses to conventions. Rising the next morning, he dropped by the newstand in the lobby, picked up a Sunday copy of The Roanoke Times, laid down his quarter and turned away.

"Wait a second!" called the lady at the newstand—"you forgot something!"

"Forgot something? What was that?" he replied.

"You have to give me a penny for the Governor!" she said.

An impish smile crossed the gubernatorial face.

"Would it be all right with you if I just give it to the Governor myself?" he inquired.

Looking at him for the first time, she broke into a hearty laugh for she recognized an almost regular customer.

The "penny for the Governor" joke soon died out across the state as people began to see the results accomplished by their pennies mounting into millions of dollars.

TAKING HIGHER EDUCATION TO THE PEOPLE

With the opening of the sixth decade of the 20th Century Virginia was becoming industrialized to a rather remarkable degree, a development which brought about increasing urban population growth which in turn demanded more attention by the State to higher education.

Industries, competing for workers, quickly discovered that there existed a discouraging lack of skilled labor and a dearth of manpower with at least two years of college education, capable of holding supervisory positions. Something had to be done.

Initially, industries took their problems to their local and state Chambers of Commerce which began wielding their influence with members of the General Assembly and with leading institutions of higher learning.

A nucleus for action already existed. The University of Virginia, Virginia Polytechnic Institute and the College of William and Mary all had excellent extension programs.

The Godwin Gesture: Then lieutenant governor, he talks with House Roads Committee.

—Richmond Newspapers Photo

In William and Mary's case, it had operated since the early 1930's the Richmond Professional Institute and its Norfolk Division which had absorbed VPI's technical school. In 1962 both were given independence by the General Assembly, RPI destined to combine with the Medical College of Virginia as Virginia Commonwealth University and Norfolk Division to become Old Dominion University with the two largest student enrollments in the state by 1969.

The 1960 Assembly, in its first effort to deal with a burgeoning problem, divided the state territorially between U. Va., W. & M. and V.P.I., permitting each to set up branch two-year colleges. The University moved into Northern Virginia, establishing George Mason College at Fairfax, raised the level of its Roanoke extension center and planned other branches at Martinsville, Lynchburg, and similar strategic locations. VPI moved into Danville, Roanoke, Wytheville and Clifton Forge. William and Mary founded Richard Bland at Petersburg and Christopher Newport at Newport News.

It quickly became apparent that this three-way split in the manner of Caesar's Gaul, wasn't going to work. U. Va. moved into Eastern Shore in W. & M. territory, into Clinch Valley in VPI territory, and a U. Va.-V.P.I. rivalry began in Roanoke.

At the 1964 General Assembly, Sen. William B. Hopkins and Del. Willis M. Anderson of Roanoke offered a bill to launch a two-year study of the situation, being especially hopeful of resolving the confrontation of two giants in their own educational front yard.

Eventually the Assembly did what they asked in the form of a resolution calling for such a study with the idea of establishing "a statewide system of comprehensive community colleges which offer post-high school education for terminal vocational and technical training and for college transfer programs of not more than two years duration".

Rather than hand this task to the Virginia Council on Higher Education, the legislators set up the Virginia Higher Education Study Commission. Governor Harrison appointed as its chairman Sen. Lloyd C. Bird, of Chesterfield, the veteran chairman of the Senate Education Committee.

The move toward such a system was not taken without misgiving. In August, addressing a meeting of the Southern Regional Education Board (SREB) at Williamsburg, Harrison expressed fears that "the expansion of community colleges will force the state to turn to private donors for aid", something which in turn would divert funds from private colleges and force them to complete the cycle by asking state assistance.

William and Mary already had been deprived of its two largest "children" and both the University of Virginia and VPI began digging in to resist any absorption of branches by the projected community college system.

Sen. Bird's committee obtained the services of Dr. John Dale Russell, Consultant on Institutional Research for Indiana University, to help with the study and writing of the report which was delivered to Gov. Harrison just before Christmas 1965. It found eleven two-year branches already in operation with the University operating Clinch Valley in VPI territory and Eastern Shore branch in the William and Mary area.

The report urged immediate consolidation of Roanoke Tech (VPI) and the University branch to end that rivalry. It suggested establishment of a State Board of Community Colleges and Technical Education controlling the new Roanoke school, U. Va's existing or planned branches on Eastern Shore, Martinsville, and Lynchburg as well as Clinch Valley while VPI was to surrender in addition to Roanoke Tech its branches at Wytheville, Danville, and Clifton Forge-Covington. U. Va's George Mason was omitted and William and Mary's Christopher Newport and Richard Bland were left in doubtful status.

There ensued in the Legislature, which witnessed Harrison's departure and Godwin's arrival, a regional struggle to exempt institutions from the new system. On February 3, before Godwin could deliver his message, the House rushed through by 93 to 1 a bill to make Clinch Valley a four-year independent college.

Before it was all over Christopher Newport had been promoted to eventual four-year status together with George Mason and Clinch Valley, giving the state the dubious distinction of having to maintain and operate 14 four-year institutions instead of 11.

On February 2, Gov. Godwin submitted his bill and, in an effort to save the system by compromise, removed Clinch Valley, Danville Tech and Richard Bland from the list subject to the Community College Board. The House, which had been playing havoc with the recommendations of the study commission, passed the Godwin measure 94 to 0.

It was at this critical juncture that dynamic young Dr. T. Marshall Hahn, president of VPI, became a strong convert to the community college idea and decided not only to alter previous tactics, which had brought about confrontation with the University of Virginia in Roanoke, but to throw his whole influence behind the Godwin plan.

Appearing before legislative committees and tirelessly stumping the state, particularly in localities where opposition had developed, he did much of the ball-carrying for the Governor. Publicly he promised to see that the VPI branches were integrated into the system as smoothly as possible.

Pressure now was against the University of Virginia and

it, too, was forced to go along, however reluctantly. Clearly this was the turning point.

Promising that the new system would mean "quality plus quantity rather than quality versus quantity", Godwin agreed to delay transfer of U. Va. and VPI branches until their proper accreditation had been assured. He also promised speedy construction with available funds.

As its first big act, the Assembly had approved a $34 million emergency appropriation bill to move up start of construction at colleges and mental hospitals by six months. Included was $1.6 million for the merging Roanoke schools which were to open as the first of a projected 23-unit system.

When the measure reached the Senate, Sen. E. Almer Ames of Eastern Shore and Sen. William F. Stone of Martinsville waged a last-ditch fight to keep University branches in their areas from being transferred to the Community College Board.

Few outside the General Assembly and the Governor have known how perilously close to the legislative rocks the whole proposal was at this moment. Determined that he would not permit it to fail, Godwin summoned Dr. Hahn; Dr. Edgar F. Shannon, president of the University of Virginia; and Dr. Davis Y. Paschall, president of the College of William and Mary, to his office on Wednesday with adjournment only three days away.

No one ever is likely to know exactly what was said that morning but there were rumors that he "laid down the law". When it was over a compromise had been reached which would leave Patrick Henry at Martinsville under the University until 1969. The Senate cleared the bill 39 to 0 and the House eventually agreed to Senate amendments, 83 to 0. Seven branches were to be transferred to the new system effective July 1 with others to be phased in gradually and the balance created.

The Governor lost little time in getting the system set up, appointing a 15-member board consisting of two-thirds businessmen and one-third educators on April 30, following this by selecting Sen. Eugene B. Sydnor as chairman and Dr. Dana B. Hamel, former head of Roanoke Tech and the State's technical school division, as director, on May 9.

The announced goal was to have 16 community colleges in operation by 1968 and all 22 by 1970. To assist the new board,

Godwin called in an advisory committee of nationally known educators from outside Virginia. The work of drafting a master plan and selecting sites on a regional basis began promptly.

The political maneuvering when the Assembly adjourned early in March had been as involved as that over the sales tax which was a necessary corollary of the overall program.

The difference was that in this instance the Governor failed to get everything he wanted. He was shocked at the idea of more state-supported four-year colleges. He had wanted every one of the branches of the larger institutions placed in the new Community College system. Again, however, he faced up to realities and struck the best bargain he could get.

When the Assembly adjourned it had enacted the sales tax and 2 per cent auto titling tax as parts of a $2.2 million budget. It had created a new $10 million parks and recreational facility program, adopted six-months daylight saving time, established at last a standard minimum driving age of 16, abolished outmoded movie censorship, repealed the state's wholesale merchant license tax, streamlined the governor's office organization and started the ball rolling toward upgrading the state's mental hospitals in addition to hundreds of lesser measures.

Well might Governor Godwin express his pride to the legislators as they adjourned: "You have moved boldly to accommodate the sound development of a growing and progressive Virginia".

As Governor Byrd had moved 40 years before to get Virginia out of the mud and start a great highway system, so now Governor Godwin had moved to jack Virginia up from its customary 42nd place in public education and begin realization of the dream of Thomas Jefferson for bringing education to the people.

How magnificently that effort fared in a scant four-year period we shall see next.

THE GOVERNOR'S CONFERENCE ON EDUCATION

Running for office in the summer and autumn of 1965, Mills Godwin had promised that, if elected, he would make education the capstone of his administration.

On December 31, only two weeks before he took over the Governor's chair, the Virginia Higher Education Study Commission, in a report largely drafted by its associate director, Dr. James R. Connor, charged that the state was not doing enough to meet its needs and that all its big institutions were located far from centers of population.

That had acted as a welcome goad to the General Assembly in pushing through the Community College system establishment and enacting the retail sales tax to help finance it as well as other school progress.

Now the Governor had what he wanted in order to attack the problems. Public schools. had been awarded $432.2 million of the new $979.98 million general fund budget with higher education receiving $116.2 million and associated agencies $23.1 million more. In addition there was $75 million for college capital outlay and teachers had been assured of $700 raises in the biennium.

He wasted little time in putting his program to work, realizing that the first task at hand was to explain to the people why the sales tax had been necessary and how the money was going to be spent.

The Virginia Association of Broadcasters was meeting at Hotel Roanoke on June 17 and, learning that the Governor had an important message he wanted to put before the public, arranged a statewide network of radio and television stations. He announced that he was calling a statewide conference on education for the early fall, its purpose to make Virginia schools as good as the best in the nation.

"Virginia has in the past jumped from crisis to crisis—plugging the dikes for next year or the year after against the flood of new knowledge and against the waves of new young people more anxious than ever to acquire that knowledge", he declared.

The time had come to reassess the past and future with its new resources, he said, adding:

"Virginians must not be swayed by any thought that Virginia cannot afford public education in modern times. The truth is nearer the axiom that Virginia cannot afford ignorance in modern times".

He hoped that the result of the conference would be a determination to "once again demonstrate Virginia's greatness and her leadership among the states".

The idea of such a conference was novel. It had never been done before. Of course, there had been state conventions of the Parent-Teacher Associations but nothing to enlist the interest, enthusiasm, brains and talent of industry, business, the professions and leaders from the non-educational world.

Unanimously, the state's press hailed the call and saw in it the launching pad for a new era in the Old Dominion.

A chief enthusiast was former Gov. Colgate W. Darden, Jr., member of the State Board of Education and former president of the University of Virginia whose great regret was that the pressures of World War II during his tenure of the governorship prevented his getting much done for education.

On August 22 at a State Board meeting in Williamsburg, Darden interrupted a "progress report" by Dr. Woodrow W. Wilkerson, state superintendent of public instruction, to warn that education gaps were widening and that "too many children in Virginia are not getting an opportunity because their schools are no good".

He demanded more progress toward quality in local systems "that can't or won't help themselves".

On September 15, with such growing support, Godwin issued his official call for the conference to be held October 5 at the Mosque in Richmond with the goal of creating "a great new wave of enthusiasm for progress in education". He chose as chairman, Virginius Dabney, editor of the Richmond Times-Dispatch, and sent out invitations to over 1,800 legislators, county, city and town officials, educators, industrialists, bankers, businessmen and professional people.

Enthusiasm mounted as the day neared and when the gavel

fell the Mosque was jammed. If it seemed like an old-fashioned revival, it was, with Governor Godwin delivering an opening address with almost religious fervor. The time was at hand, he said, when something had to be done. One almost could hear the "amens" from the far balcony.

Virginians, he said, "with hardly a murmur of protest shouldered a major new tax, the first in more than a century, believing these revenues would flow into our schools and colleges, filling in still more of their shortcomings, relieving still more of their limitations, broadening all of their possibilities".

"We will fall into catastrophic error if we rest now, assuming the major part of our work is done", he said, warning localities against reducing their share of school support. He recalled Jefferson's bitter defeat by the General Assembly of his dream of public education. He reminded his audience that when William Barton Rogers, the great scientist from William and Mary, pleaded in vain for just $15,000 to open a pioneer school of applied science, Rogers went north and founded the Massachusetts Institute of Technology.

"Today men of vision once more are pleading with us on behalf of every schoolboy, every undergraduate, every graduate and every post-graduate student. And what will our answer be? Will we turn away? Will we cheer from a safe distance? Or will we plunge into the work nearest our hand?" he challenged.

"Together let us kindle an evangelical fire and let us keep it bright until it ignites the faintest hearts and warms the coldest feet!"

In a morning session devoted to the public schools the hardest hitting was done by Thomas C. Boushall, chairman of the board of the Bank of Virginia, who laid into the state's record with a broadsword of statistics, observing that "Virginia has no way to go but up!"

The state, he said, while 14th in population was 34th in income but in the lowest quarter in every significant category, such as 45th in per capita tax collections and 47th in percentage of those voting in presidential elections.

Until the gaps are closed, he contended, Virginia would never recover the place of primacy it once held but that it did have the "economic muscle" to do the job.

The Press Conference where Godwin was usually in good form. Here he tells reporters some fine points of his program.

Then Boushall created a sensation with his proposal that the state Constitution "should be promptly amended to permit the issuance of bonds limited to use in public educational affairs".

It was a trial balloon, recalling the legislative proposal of Sen. William B. Hopkins and Del. Willis M. Anderson of Roanoke in 1964 to scrap pay-as-we-go and issue bonds, and destined to launch a statewide debate, culminating in the constitutional amendments.

If the morning session appealed to public school supporters, it was the afternoon program centering on higher education which captured imaginations.

With Dr. Perry Kendig, president of Roanoke College presiding, a panel composed of Dr. T. Marshall Hahn, president of VPI; Dr. Edgar F. Shannon, president of the University of

101

Virginia; and Dr. Davis Y. Paschall, president of William and Mary, shored up the Godwin position on institutional needs.

Predicting a two-thirds jump in college age population to 350,000 in a decade, Dr. Hahn told the huge crowd that Virginia had no choice but to enlarge and strengthen graduate programs. He added:

"We must build a community college system which will bring post high school educational opportunities within commuting distance of every Virginia youth".

Substantially more revenue was needed to put Old Dominion graduate level education into the front rank, Dr. Shannon asserted.

It is, he said, "essential to the research and development that provide new knowledge and methods, which, translated into products and techniques, vitally affect our ability to compete in a dynamic and rapidly changing technology".

Dr. Paschall for his part warned that the state should not relegate undergraduate liberal arts programs to a cushion between high school and college and opposed too early specialization.

Saying that community colleges would have a broadened opportunity, he observed that "other colleges must turn quickly to the task of preparing teachers for them and aiding them in every consultative way possible".

"If we are now capable of reaching into space, we must liberally educate for true worthiness in moving among the stars", he concluded.

Those who filled the Mosque that day had caught the vision the Governor had hoped for and as they adjourned they adopted a resolution urging that he hold regional conferences in every part of the state.

The state's press redoubled its enthusiasm editorially and almost immediately Godwin began setting up machinery for informative meetings during February and March in Richmond, Farmville, Bristol, Roanoke, Fredericksburg, Alexandria, Harrisonburg and Norfolk.

The Governor attended each one, sounding the keynote that the sales tax was vital to a proper expanding educational program. It was, concluded Melville Carico, veteran political reporter of The Roanoke Times, a superb job of building grass roots support not only for his program but for the legislators who had helped him put it on the books.

Exclaimed The Roanoke World-News: (March 11) "Never before has a Virginia governor tackled the needs and shortcomings of public education on school and college levels with such imagination and vigor. Mr. Godwin deserves the gratitude of every citizen for first class leadership. When the 1968 General Assembly convenes it should have a geen light for progress".

On October 5 that year, Godwin stressed that the education budget must get top priority in the 1968 General Assembly in order to complete the job that had been started.

The next four days Williamsburg played host to the International Conference on the World Crisis in Education with President Johnson and Gov. Godwin as two of the principal speakers.

By the end of the year the State Board of Education was moving to compel consolidation of tiny rural schools in order to carry out the Godwin determination to bring quality education to children of the Commonwealth no matter how remote their homes or how poor their counties.

And to complete his satisfaction, the community college program was in full swing. He was ready for the next step.

CONFRONTATION WITH THE KLAN

One of the strangest phenomena in the South since the Civil War has been the periodic revival of the Ku Klux Klan as an expression of white supremacy in areas with heavy Negro population.

Usually it has been a far cry from the organization of hooded night riders identified in Reconstruction days with Gen. Nathan Bedford Forest (old 'Git thar fustest with the mostes') and elevated to heroic stature by D. W. Griffith when he filmed "The Klansmen" as part of "The Birth of a Nation".

103

Now, About That Klan . . . The Governor minced no words when he talked of the sheeted brethren.

At one time, in the 1920's, a new Klan became virtually nationwide in its scope and appeal. On one occasion more than 10,000 hooded and be-sheeted brethren with their ladies auxiliary marched down Pennsylvania Avenue in Washington, D. C.

It was about this time that a huge statewide rally in Williamsburg insisted on giving and dedicating a flagpole to the College of William and Mary. President J. A. C. Chandler felt compelled to accept but refused to have it on the ancient main campus. Students subsequently removed the plaque and after a short time the flag was never flown from the pole again.

After some its national officials ran afoul of the law in the 1930's and found themselves in prison, the greatest Klan revival gradually died away. It was rather obvious that its power waned in almost direct proportion to the increase of public education.

It was inevitable, of course, that bigotry and racism should spring to new flower in parts of rural Virginia as in the other rural South in the wake of the U. S. Supreme Court's public school desegregation decision of May 17, 1954 and subsequent efforts to integrate hitherto all-white schools.

The Klan gained new strength after President Eisenhower sent troops into Little Rock. President Johnson's efforts to enforce the decision added fuel to the fire despite the fact that he had carried Virginia in 1964. The fact that Governor Godwin had spoken for LBJ and had ridden the "Ladybird Special" made him despised by the Klan. It was inevitable that they should clash.

In the fall of 1966, a year after his election, Godwin was still the target of denunciation at Klan rallies as school integration heated up again. All across rural Southside and in some other areas crosses were being burned, often on the front lawns of black militants and white moderates and liberals.

Grand Dragon of the Virginia Klan was Marshall Kornegay, of North Carolina, with Charles Elder, of South Hill, second in command.

The Klan was whipping up sentiment among the ignorant and gullible. It did not always have permits for its rallies on private property after use of public property had been denied. It was making considerable money from the sale of paraphernalia. Harranguing spokesmen were making promises they could not keep and taped recordings made by authorities proved some rather serious threats against the President and the Governor.

Godwin, who hated the Klan with a passion, denounced it and its spokesmen on several occasions.

On the night of December 8 Capitol Police discovered a cross burning on the sidewalk below the wall-fence in the rear of the Mansion and saw a man run to a car and speed away.

The Governor and a friend, Del. Edward E. Lane of Richmond, had flown to Memphis to watch VPI in the Liberty Bowl game but Mrs. Godwin, Mrs. Lane and the Godwin's daughter, Becky, were at home. Fortunately, although hearing some commotion, they were not aware of what happened.

This cowardly act under cover of darkness infuriated the Governor to whom an appropriate forum opened a few nights later when he addressed the Conference of Christians and Jews in Richmond.

He announced that as of then he would pursue a tough

policy, that cross burnings of this sort were a felony, that every state facility would be employed to track down, apprehend and prosecute offenders and that a $1,000 reward would be paid for information leading to arrests and convictions.

The public supported the Governor and information came in. Several offenders were tried and convicted. One Richmond jury "threw the book" at one man and sent him to prison for three years.

In February 1967, two months after the Mansion cross burning, Grand Dragon Kornegay asked for a conference with the Governor for himself and Elder.

The day before the scheduled conference, Godwin went to Moneta in Bedford to dedicate a new garment plant owned by Roanoke interests and was advised by the local sheriff that there was word of Klan plans to burn a cross at the ceremonies.

As it turned out, the cross-burners got jittery and set their fire early but the cross was still smoking near a filling station across the road from the new plant when the Governor arrived. He made the speech and roasted the Klan and its cowardice.

The incident served to strengthen his hand when Kornegay and Elder appeared the next day. Also present were Carter O. Lowance, commissioner of administration; John Wessells, press secretary and Mrs. Pat Perkinson, the Governor's executive assistant.

Kornegay, described by Godwin as a tall, handsome man of unusually fluent speech, disclaimed responsibility for the cross burnings, complained of police harassment and asked for protection of the Klan rallies.

Hearing the Grand Dragon out and discovering that Elder had nothing to add, Godwin proceeded to lay down the law in a voice which displayed his anger as well as his contempt for the Klan.

There had been no harassment, he said, but it was his duty and obligation to enforce the law and, if necessary, he would use all 800 State troopers and would not hesitate to employ the National Guard to break the back of the Klan in Virginia.

That confrontation appeared to have been what was needed to halt the upsurge of the Klan. Both men stated their sides to the press and there ensued a mounting support of the Governor.

106

"From that day forward the back of the Klan in Virginia was truly broken", recalls Godwin with a note of pride in his voice.

Gradually the rallies of robed and hooded figures dwindled and the cross-burnings flickered out even in Southside. It was no longer the smart thing to belong in some rural circles.

As Harry Byrd had put an end to lynchings 40 years before by throwing all the power of the Commonwealth into his fight against a despicable evil, so Mills Godwin by firm leadership relegated a hateful symbol of a darker age to the limbo.

There has been no revival.

THE GOVERNOR AS A SALESMAN

The Old Dominion's New Era was never better epitomized than by the alliance of Governor Godwin with the business, industrial, trade and travel interests of the State.

After putting his 1966 legislative program through the General Assembly and superintending the job of seeing that it functioned, he became Virginia's first super-salesman both at home and abroad.

The Byrd Organization had always been noted for its friendly attitude toward business for the Senior Senator was a business-man himself who started at the age of 14 and never forgot it. There never was much need for big campaign kitties because there was no opposition within or without the party that was worth mention. But such financial support as the Organization required it could be sure of getting from the state's business, industrial, banking and professional circles.

Until the close of World War II, however, the Commonwealth never did much for business and industry except to regu-late it with an even-tempered hand through the State Corporation

Commission. Of course, there was a reasonable effort to support trade and tourism with emphasis on the highway program but nothing of a high pressure nature.

As a matter of fact, the Organization was a political thing which welcomed support if it was of the "right" kind but it never made any real attempt to become a partner of business. Being rural-based, for its strength centered around the courthouses, it may not have frowned on industrial promotion but it certainly did not go out of its way. Too much industry meant too much unionization and fundamentally the interests of factory labor were not those of agricultural and rural Virginia.

Emphasis during the governorship of William M. Tuck had been on the "right-to-work" laws. John S. Battle was determined to emphasize better public schools. Thomas B. Stanley, first businessman governor since Byrd, brought beginnings of a new interest in industry but J. Lindsay Almond, Jr. became enmeshed in Massive Resistance and had little time for anything else.

Albertis S. Harrison thus became the first governor in 20 years to have much time for business promotion. One of his earliest acts was to set up an advisory board for Industrial Development with Sen. Harry F. Byrd, Jr. as chairman, its task being to coordinate state activities in this field and help to recruit business.

Byrd having gone to the U. S. Senate, Governor Godwin promptly appointed Harrison as chairman of that body and retained all of his predecessor's 11-man board.

Godwin early indicated to the General Assembly that he wanted to put emphasis on expanding the economic base of the State and gradually his program took shape. It concentrated on three main phases—industrial development at home, foreign trade and tourism.

Although a product of a rural-oriented political organization, he realized that the face of Virginia was changing and that it had to change more if it was going to compete with North Carolina, Florida and other sister-states of the Old South.

Virginia already had a comparatively stable market of high-grade labor and a sound taxation system to commend it. Also the quality of its public schools had been improving steadily and the progress of higher education was insured by approval of a new

Community College system. In addition there were countless fine industrial sites, plenty of water and good year-around climate.

With such material, Governor Godwin's talents of speaking and persuasion were put to work. He made four annual trips to New York City where as many as 400 representatives of management with branches in Virginia were luncheon guests of the Virginia State Chamber of Commerce and transplanted Virginians.

On the same trips he spoke to large gatherings of travel writers, it being in his language "a wonderful opportunity to brag about Virginia". The results included many industrial leads and numerous feature stories in metropolitan papers and the big magazines.

There have been similar annual excursions to Chicago which also produced results not in goodwill alone.

Invaluable in "showing the state" to industrial leaders and in enabling the Governor to participate often in critical negotiations for a plant was the new 8-passenger Beechcraft airplane, acquired in 1968.

With such help for the diligent efforts of the State and local chambers of commerce, results were nothing short of amazing. In three years industrial growth exceeded the previous four years with total expenditures of $1.06 billion compared to $1.017 billion.

The number of new plants jumped from 295 in the 1962-66 period to 380 in 1966-68 with plant expansions numbering around 340 in each period and with new jobs ranging from 43,800 to 46,500.

Conference: Godwin talks with President W. H. Bowditch of the Virginia State Chamber of Commerce as Chamber staff members listen. From left, Mrs. Dirk van Meeteren Brouwer, Miss Elizabeth Mathewson, Miss Mary Lillian Shelton and Mrs. Gordon W. Jones.

—Virginia State Chamber of Commerce Photo

For the first time during the Godwin adminstration Virginia got around to spending a minimum of $1 million on travel promotion and advertising and it paid off. By 1969 tourism was generating $840 million a year in revenue. The State could well afford to open a tourist information center in Rockefeller Center, New York, as well as in Richmond.

In four years the industry responded by spending $100 million on new travel accomodations.

For the past two years new industries or enlargement of existing plants have averaged one a week with initial outlays of $10 million to $20 million not unusual. All of which has broadened the state's economic base, created new jobs with higher pay, more state and local tax revenue and adding hundreds of new citizens per week.

The high water mark came in 1969 when the British-based Imperial Chemical Company came to Chesterfield County with an opening outlay of $50 million, largest in Virginia history, and the great Anheuser Busch Co. of St. Louis announced plans to build a $40 million brewery and later a tourist garden, industrial park and a residential project in James City County near Williamsburg.

It was in the foreign trade market, however, that Governor Godwin was to make the Old Dominion's biggest publicity splash.

The State had been exporting tobacco since John Rolfe started it all 350 years ago and it is still a considerable item. Coal, however, long since achieved first place with the opening of bituminous fields in Western Virginia and West Virginia, hauled to Hampton Roads by the Norfolk & Western and Chesapeake & Ohio railways. The flow increases 10 per cent annually.

There are many other exports, of course. For example, at least 10 per cent of General Electric's industrial control equipment goes abroad. In 1966 it was estimated that 375 Virginia firms had foreign trade of at least $500 million.

It was in October of that year that Godwin announced he would lead a party of 33 businessmen to Europe in the Spring of 1967 to tell the Virginia story and try to promote trade through Hampton Roads were the State Ports Authority was trying to develop full potentials of one of the world's greatest natural harbors.

110

The Well Dressed Virginian: To show what could be done, the State Chamber of Commerce sent Governor Godwin to a meeting completely clothed in Virginia-made articles ranging from underwear to topcoat and from hat to shoes. Here he enjoys the game with Richard S. Gillis, Jr., executive director, and W. H. Bowditch, president of the Chamber.

The Ports Authority already had George McKinney operating in Brussels while the State Department of Agriculture was soon to add Conrad Lutz, promoting livestock and both were doing a good job.

Leaving Dulles International Airport on March 28 in a gesture toward developing greater use of that northern Virginia facility, the first European Trade Mission visited Spain, Italy, Sweden and Belgium.

With the Governor went his chief aide, Carter Lowance; Maurice Rowe, the commissioner of agriculture, and J. Eldred Hill, director of the Division of Development, plus representatives of outstanding industries of the state. Everybody paid his own way.

In each country they were greeted by high officials of government, including King Gustav VI of Sweden and Premier Paul Van den Boeynants of Belgium. It was the first venture by any state into what was called "face-to-face business diplomacy". The Europeans were both flattered and pleased.

Notable was the audience with 84-year-old King Gustav who showed himself well acquainted with American history and they discussed seafood research and ocean currents, especially the Gulf

Stream which flows past Virginia and ultimately helps make Sweden and all Scandinavia habitable. They gave him a Williamsburg tea caddy.

In Brussels, as elsewhere, they toured industrial plants, as they combined sight-seeing with business contacts (over 500 in all) and got numerous firm orders for everything from furniture to metals.

Reporting later, Godwin predicted dividends would flow in many ways, that "many firms were anxious to begin immediate affiliation" and that orders were "far in excess of what I expected them to be".

One of his party, Donald L. Jordan, chairman of the board of Johnson-Carper Furniture Co. and a veteran traveler, lauded the Governor for doing "a wonderful job", expressed the belief that Virginia could compete with the European Common Market, and reported that a visit to Williamsburg seemed to be a common ambition among business and governmental leaders abroad.

Encouraged by this initial foray, Godwin asked the 1968 General Assembly for funds to establish a foreign trade office, which was done, and a new mission planned for 1969 to open it.

Soon after the first trip, Mr. Hill resigned and Godwin named J. Frank Alspaugh as director of industrial development. At the same time, by executive order, he directed that division, the State Ports Authority and the Department of Agriculture to coordinate their activities on foreign trade. All three now are represented in the Brussels office.

By 1969 Hampton Roads had become second only to New York for containerized transshipments abroad.

There followed annual World Trade conferences, the one in Norfolk in 1967 taking stock of the Godwin mission and urging 350 more firms to get in the export trade. An export workshop in Roanoke opposed the imposition of U. S. quotas lest there be retaliation.

In August 1968, Dennis E. Ruffin was appointed European director of the new International Trade and Development section of the Virginia Division of Industrial Development. With experience in Belgium and Luxemburg, he joined Conrad Lutz in the Brussels office.

In late April, 1969, Governor Godwin headed his second

European Trade Mission out of Dulles Airport, the party swollen this time to 110 by the presence of wives.

Again they visited Belgium where he cut the ribbon to open the State's new trade offices in Brussels and they were received by Prince Albert, brother of King Baudoin, and by Prime Minister Gaston Eysken.

The Governor and some of the party then went to Spain where, among other things, they visited a 20,000 acre cattle ranch and Godwin had a street named for him in the town nearby.

An industrial group went to Zurich, Switzerland. They then met in Antwerp and visited in England and West Germany. It was while they were in London that Fred G. Kessner, the state's foreign trade director, announced that a large European firm would build a plant in Virginia.

Altogether 198 business calls were made with 35 being rated as good for immediate action and 39 for future potential.

The two trade missions were known to have inspired numerous other business trips by groups and individuals to nearly all the countries of Europe and even as far away as Australia.

In all the stops where Godwin participated there was a pleased and sometimes even surprised reaction as Europeans learned that an individual American state was promoting business without the inspiration or assistance of the federal government. That the head of one of the best known states should take the trouble to lead the delegation impressed them tremendously.

As for the Governor, he was entitled to an exuberant spirit over the success and his enthusiasm was understandable when he told a gathering of business leaders in Roanoke that FFV now means "First Firms of Virginia".

For them and the Governor it had become a happy partnership.

After close of the "Constructive Session" of the General Assembly in late March, 1966—a short gathering of leadership for the purpose of signing bills—Governor Godwin had the remainder of that year and 1967 in which to put the machinery of his program to work. At the heart of it, of course, was the matter of making the sales tax effective.

As usual for governors, he had to start planning in the spring of 1967 for the 1968-70 biennial budget to be submitted to the next General Assembly regular session in January, 1968.

Together with a budget study commission composed of legislators and state officials, he toured institutions and listened to their pleas for operating and capital funds. While pleased with the additional money available from the sales tax, he was aware, as had been every predecessor, that there still wasn't enough to do everything which needed doing.

"It was necessary to nail down and to secure the gains that had been made in the 1966 session. I wanted to see Virginia's forward thrust continued," he explained.

"Pay-as-you-go had been in effect over 40 years and if anything was sacred around this state, this certainly was. I had been an adherent of it but I thought the time had come that we had to do something. It did not seem possible for the state to continue its progress unless we made changes, especially as concerned capital outlays and buildings that had to be constructed.

"The requests were many and we were unable to meet them by more than $300 million in preparation for the 1968-70 budget. And so, I decided that I would ask the General Assembly for authority to hold a referendum and let the people say whether the borrowing authority for general obligation debt as provided in the Constitution might now be exercised".

The proposal was made to a joint session of Senate and House along with a $3.1 billion budget with a theme of "New Dimensions for Virginia".

While current revenues could be expected to finance operating costs, they could provide for only a fraction of capital needs. Consequently, he incorporated a proposal which was to mark the final break with the old pay-as-you-go system and simultaneously abolish what had been both fetish and rallying banner of the Byrd Machine.

He called for approval of a referendum to authorize state bonds totalling $70.8 million—The major portion for college construction including the community college system created in 1966 and the rest for new construction at mental hospitals.

To understand fully the significance of the Godwin proposal it is necessary to review some Virginia history.

Debt had been an evil word for more than a century, indeed going back to building of the James River and Kanawha Canal, which had its inception when George Washington still lived.

Railroads and floods killed the canals and about all the Commonwealth has to show of a worthy nature even to this day is some very profitable stock in the Richmond, Fredericksburg and Potomac Railroad. This little "gold mine" is vigorously protected although hardly a legislative session goes by that someone does not propose selling the stock to pay for some improvement.

The Federal Government, of course, declared debts of the Confederacy null and void after the Civil War, but Virginia had a debt of its own which the majority, at least among politicians, considered "sacred." It amounted to more than $45 million and interest alone constituted a big item in the budget every year.

There is no room here to recite details of the bitter postwar, Reconstruction and Readjuster eras stretching from 1865 to the 1902 constitutional convention, but that debt dominated public thinking for nearly 100 years.

Not until the subject had been threshed out before the U. S. Supreme Court in the middle of the 20th Century did West Virginia agree to pay its proportionate share of pre-war debt. It was long after Mills Godwin entered the General Assembly that the last bond was paid off.

Harry Flood Byrd, whose father, Richard Evelyn Byrd, was Speaker of the House of Delegates, had been born into this atmosphere as well as one of family struggles against bankruptcy

115

and was only 15 years old when the 1902 Constitution was proclaimed.

Frugality and living within one's means had been basic principles from early youth. Like every man who became governor, he dreamed of paying off that debt. Having the money in a sinking fund to pay the bonds as they came due was an obsession.

Thus it was that, as a young State Senator, he fought against the proposal to issue $50 million in bonds to build highways, following the example of neighboring North Carolina. His idea prevailed in the 1923 referendum and two years later he defeated G. Walter Mapp as the champion of pay-as-you-go.

In the subsequent constitutional revisions setting up Byrd's far-reaching modernization of the governmental structure in 1926-28, he saw to it that there was one small "escape valve" to provide for issuance of bonds in an emergency.

Although real estate was transferred exclusively to localities as a revenue source under the tax segregation act, it was stipulated that the State might issue bonds equal to one per cent of the total of assessed value of real estate in Virginia but only by approval of the people.

Godwin and his fiscal advisors now estimated that this clause would permit issuance of up to $81 million in bonds although he would ask for only $70.8 million and leaving a reasonable margin.

Once the idea caught on in the Assembly enthusiasm mounted with the result that it decided, on recommendation of committees, to ask authorization of the entire $81 million. The vote, strictly on party lines, was 74 to 20 in the House and 28 to 7 in the Senate.

There was no question about the need. Normal economic growth was expected to bring in an additional $200 million. The sales tax was producing better than expected and by now the wisdom was clear in the 1966 decision to provide an automatic boost of one per cent effective July 1, 1968.

In addition, in Godwin's words, Tax Commissioner Morrissett "pulled the last rabbit out of the hat" by suggesting that payment of witholding taxes and certain corporation taxes be accelerated to produce a one-time $61 million windfall.

After some sparring, the Assembly went along with that, too, and in the end the $3.13 billion appropriations act, including

116

Oh, My Aching Budget! Governor Godwin holds his head in mock anguish as Budget Director L. M. Kuhn presents the 1968-70 budget, or what has to go into it. Despite its precarious height, it balanced as Virginia budgets always must.

$81 million for bonds, was passed despite the vigorous protest of a leading Republican, Sen. J. Kenneth Robinson, that this meant the death of pay-as-you-go.

There was $31 million available for capital work in the general budget and this, plus $81 million from bonds, if approved, would meet most immediate needs but Godwin foresaw that the constitutional limit on bonds must be liberalized.

There had been no significant changes in the Constitution since Byrd's time in the governorship. Godwin promised that if the Assembly would agree, he would appoint a blue ribbon commission to conduct a study and make recommendations to a special legislative session in 1969.

He pointed out that whatever amendments were suggested must receive approval of two successive legislatures so that whatever was passed in 1969 must also get endorsement in 1970 before it could be submitted to the people in referendum.

Almost unanimously, but with some Republican objection, this also cleared both houses and Godwin acted almost immediately, appointing as chairman former Gov. Harrison whom he had named to the Supreme Court of Appeals upon the retirement of Justice C. Vernon Spratley of Hampton in the summer of 1967.

It was notable that by mid-session just about all of the major legislation sought by Godwin had been enacted with almost unheard of alacrity. Indeed, so swift was the action that the legislators were widely accused of "coasting" the last month.

At one point the Governor had to revise upward by $22 million his estimated sales tax revenue when a federal court decision forbade the State to withhold aid from localities receiving "impacted area" funds because of the presence of federal military installations.

Even so, spending for schools overall was up 28 per cent above the 1966-68 biennium. It gave teachers a $600 raise over the next two years, raised state aid per pupil to $110 and $115 in those years, boosted the total school appropriations by $161 million, launched a local option kindergarten program, provided for seven more community colleges, allocated money to upgrade college faculty salaries, reenacted compulsory school attendance and set up a two-year study of free text books but refused to abolish tuition grants. The last action didn't matter a great deal because the courts soon disposed of that.

In addition, it merged Richmond Professional Institute and the Medical College of Virginia to create a new Virginia Commonwealth University and elevated Clinch Valley College to a four-year, degree-granting institution.

About the only defeat for the Governor, if we could call it that, was the rather thorough emasculation of the series of bills growing out of the report of the Metropolitan Areas Study Commission headed by Dr. T. Marshall Hahn, president of VPI.

118

There was widespread fear that some of the proposals, if enacted, would put too much control over local government at the State Capitol. As a result, the main accomplishments were creation of regional planning districts and provision for consolidation of cities with counties, counties with counties and counties with towns.

The one major battle in which Godwin took no part was over the proposal to expand Virginia's successful 34-year-old Alcoholic Beverage Control Act to permit serving of liquor-by-the-drink in food establishments. His only role was to help block the idea of a statewide referendum and final action was to put it on a strictly local option basis. He didn't want it on the ballot with college and hospital bonds but many localities put it there anyhow without harm to his pet project, as we shall see in another chapter.

Among other things, the 1968 Assembly enacted a strong riot control law providing for local and interstate shifting of police and national guard, enacted a tough "habitual offender" act to clamp down on bad drivers, and passed a "truth in lending" law.

Mindful of Judge Morrissett's warning about exhaustion of tax sources, it set up a commission to study new sources and provided for another commission to look into election laws. Remembering Godwin's experiences with the Klan, it also put on the books a law making cross-burning on public or unauthorized private property a crime.

It increased maximum payments for unemployment insurance and workmen's compensation but killed unceremoniously the back-door effort of Sen. Henry E. Howell, Jr. to have the "agency shop" legalized.

It appropriated $20 million to help get Medicaid started but with well-nigh unanimous lack of enthusiasm. It also enacted a "freedom of information" law with a hole so big that Attorney General Button subsequently drove a truck through it.

And finally, without knowing it would be for a Republican's benefit, the legislators raised the salary of the next Governor to $35,000 a year.

So outstanding was the 1968 General Assembly that Lt. Gov. Fred Pollard called it "probably the hardest working in this

119

century". Taking note of Godwin's record, he added: "Mr. Godwin forged his own organization by the sheer weight of his personality and his exhibition of determination".

All of which was true, but Godwin was leaving to his successor a tremendous problem of financing any new programs beyond those in effect when a new decade dawned.

HOW DECISIONS ARE MADE

How did you decide to do that?

Here was a question frequently asked of men in public life, especially governors who must formulate policy.

It may seem strange to some people, but Mills Godwin reached a lot of his important decisions just walking around. Around the Capitol grounds, that is.

Of course, he had a fairly well designed plan of action when he first came to office and it was a good thing that he did because there wasn't much opportunity to do anything but work those first three months.

But, as he settled into the routine of office, some regular form of exercise became a necessity and walking around Capitol Square's brick and concrete sidewalks which meander up and down hill became something of a nightly routine.

Sometimes he walked alone, sometimes with a Capitol policeman—the police always had him in sight, as he discovered when he ducked behind a tree to test the security.

Godwin recalls with a chuckle the old story of how Governor "Big Bill" Tuck is reported to have walked out on the grounds one night and fired a pistol several times to check reactions. According to the story, it was quite some time before anyone arrived to investigate and the Governor felt this was rather poor protection for one of the most historical and valuable properties in America.

Whatever the facts, there now is a Capitol Police force of 20 men assigned to a 24-hour patrol, guarding not only the

Capitol but the Mansion. One is on duty at the Mansion gate day and night and one stays in the basement at night, routinely checking the first floor. With Capt. W. A. Seawell in command, they chauffeur the Governor and his family if a State Trooper is not available and, so far as the Godwins are concerned "were a part of our family".

Godwin counted his steps over various routes and discovered that twice around one way was equal to a mile and a quarter. Often he made three rounds or more. Often he paused to commune with statues of the great inside and outside the Capitol.

Ever Talk With a Statue? Governor Godwin frequently paused to consult images of Virginia greats as he walked the Capitol grounds, thinking out his decisions.

"These walks gave me a sense of history", he says. "I never passed the great equestrian statue of Washington surrounded by other great Virginians like Patrick Henry, George Rogers Clark and John Marshall, or the statues of Stonewall Jackson, Dr. Henry Hunter McGuire, or Governor William Smith without experiencing this peculiar sensation.

"Or I would go inside to contemplate that marvelous Houdon statue of Washington surrounded by busts of Lafayette and the other seven Virginia-born Presidents, or step into the old hall of the House of Delegates and stand by the statue of Lee there on the exact spot where he took command of the Army of Virginia, and have the feeling of challenge and comfort.

"It was a great inspiration. All around the Capitol on four sides the towering office buildings would be lighted and there was the sound of traffic outside but here was a quietness and stillness that did something to me. At times I was almost talking to myself about what I wanted to do for this State, what programs I was planning, what actions would be taken.

"I was never more conscious of this than during such walks in the fall and winter of 1967 as I approached the opening of the 1968 General Assembly. I was trying to get the budget ready and make a decision I knew history might have something to say about—the pay-as-you-go plan and what to do about additional revenue. I knew I could not ask for more taxes. The more I thought, the more it was inescapable that I must request the General Assembly to ask the people for a bond issue to make capital improvements.

"It was not an easy decision. I had always supported pay-as-you-go. To leave it and choose another course was going to set our sails on uncharted seas and I knew it would have some repercussion in certain quarters because it represented a major departure from our policy since 1928.

"The walks gave me the inner strength to set my course and make the proposal for general obligation debt. Coupled with this was the fact that I was going to propose a Commission on Constitutional Revision that would set in motion machinery that would provide for further enlarging of the debt".

Before launching any of his programs, Godwin consulted leaders of the General Assembly in depth, for "a governor must have support to get action", he says, "and I probably spent more time at it than any of my predecessors, especially with the conservatives. It paid rich dividends".

Occasionally, too, he contacted friends of key legislators to enlist their influence. And he always had his staff and departmental heads at his call when wanted for counsel.

Yet, there are many times when a Governor can be lonely in the very heart of a great city, even with his family close by and knowing that he has the best of expert advice. In the end, the decisions are his alone to make.

Mills Godwin regards the 1968 General Assembly as one of the best in Virginia history and, so far as he is concerned, the most statesmanlike of his career.

Sometimes, mainly on Sunday afternoons, the Governor's strolls occured in daytime and it was often that he came upon visitors standing, looking in awe at the Capitol or staring at the Mansion.

It was then that he interrupted his chain of thought to pause for a handshake with startled but pleased tourists. Not infrequently he invited them into the Mansion or into the garden—a lovely little oasis—or guided a group around the Capitol, reciting the history he knew so well. Especially he liked to play host to children.

The Mansion is a home which belongs to the people of Virginia, he says, and a treasure that is not to be abused, but he wishes it were possible for more to see it. He has many letters in his files from visitors, particularly from out-of-state, expressing appreciation for his impromptu tours. This has earned immense goodwill.

The Mansion is open annually for Virginia Historic Garden Week and some groups are received by special appointment. The Tobacco Festival Queen and her princesses are regularly received each fall.

The Executive Mansion, erected in 1813 and housing every governor since that date, is no museum piece but a beautiful home with swan fountain and lovely private garden.

About the only other recreation Governor Godwin had besides his regular walks (there wasn't too much exercise watching baseball games no matter how he loved them) was found on summer vacations at Camp Pendleton or on a weekend of salt water fishing, a delight since boyhood on the Nansemond river.

Cruising and fishing on the "Chesapeake" or some other boat of the Virginia Fisheries Commission also gave time for thinking. As Isaac Walton testified, much of man's best thinking is done while wetting a line, although Isaac preferred lolling on a riverbank to fishing from a boat.

Especially did Godwin love fishing off Eastern Shore. In 1967 off Oyster with Claude Rogers he caught a citation fish—a 112-pound shark—which he turned over to local people for a picnic being held the next day. Some of his favorite fishing companions were Milton T. Hickman, commissioner of the Marine Resources Department, Charlie Bagnell, Talmadge Scott, Gordon Brooks, G. Clayton Shoemaker and Capt. Edgar Miles of Willis Wharf.

The Governor always returned to Richmond loaded down with salt water wisdom and far more fish than three Godwins could eat. Consequently, the Mansion staff shared the over-supply and there were never too many.

Sometimes it is best not to think too much and it was on such occasions that he and Becky (occasionally Mrs. Godwin) went to watch the Richmond Braves, a farm of Atlanta, perform.

The management always had a box for them and, like other fans, they sated themselves with peanuts. popcorn, hot dogs and soft drinks. Each of his four gubernatorial years Godwin tossed out the first ball to start the season and conjured up memories of his own ball-playing days in youth. To keep the memories alive, he puchased boxes of baseballs which he loved to autograph and give to youngsters who visited his office.

But much of the time Godwin had to get his sports via the television tube like millions of fellow Americans.

SUMMER OF FUN AND POLITICS

The summer of 1968 had been a happy time for Becky Godwin who was to achieve her fifteenth birthday on September 7.

As soon as classes were over at St. Catherine's she went to Camp Sequoya for five weeks and it was a deeply tanned young lady, glowing with youthful energy, who greeted her parents when they arrived to take her home.

But first they saw her perform in the ski show, had dinner together and then drove to Mountain Empire Airport at Groseclose near Marion from where the new state plane whisked them back to Richmond.

The National Governors Conference was approaching at Cincinnati and this time she wanted to go because there were reports of wonderful things planned for the children such as boat rides on the Ohio, swimming, picnics and dancing. She had a great time.

President and Mrs. Johnson came for the State dinner where he spoke and meeting them was a thrill for the young girl.

Maybe even more fun was dancing with the Governor of Virginia to the music of Guy Lombardo and demonstrating for him what she had been learning at the Cotillion Club.

It was a fun break Mills Godwin needed, too, because there were ahead the State Democratic Convention at Salem and then the National Convention in Chicago, neither of which he relished particularly.

As Governor, he was temporary chairman of the State Convention and it proved to be, in his language, "one of the rowdiest I've ever attended" and "much of it a disgrace to the party".

The liberal elements clustered around State Sen. Henry E. Howell, Jr. of Norfolk, tried to stampede the convention, the tactics of delegations from the Second and Eighth districts being especially distasteful to Godwin. His antipathy toward Howell seemed to ripen from that time.

As temporary chairman and keynoter, he suffered through most of a brawling day and finally was able to hand the gavel to

Speaker John Warren Cooke, the permanent chairman, at 7:30 in the evening.

Godwin's candidate for reelection as State Chairman, Rep. Watkins Abbitt, finally won over Joseph T. Fitzpatrick of Norfolk, a Howell lieutenant and the Senator's campaign manager in the 1969 primaries.

The Governor saw in Abbitt's victory "the insurance of some stability for the party" although the liberal wing managed to gain a measure of control.

It was a tired Godwin who was to head for Chicago on Aug. 24 for convening of the National Convention two days later amid threatened violent disorder and conflict between liberals and conservatives.

Virginia had decided to go along with Vice President Hubert H. Humphrey as the presidential candidate, hoping to gain with the aid of other Southern States a more moderate running mate. As leader of the delegation, Godwin faced a rugged, uphill road.

Before he went, however, Mrs. Godwin was to undergo serious abdominal surgery at Norfolk General Hospital. With Becky they spent the weekend on the "Chesapeake", the State Fisheries boat, getting some rest and just enjoying being together.

Mrs. Godwin entered the hospital on Monday, August 12, and underwent successful surgery the following Wednesday.

The Governor and Becky stayed close by in the cottage provided for the chief executive at Camp Pendleton, summer home of the Virginia National Guard. It was something of a joke to them that four members of the Mansion staff were waiting on just two people.

For the ten days between Mrs. Godwin's operation and her release for recuperation, father and daughter had a wonderful time together—what was probably their longest and closest association, just swimming, walking the beach, relaxing and occasionally going to Virginia Beach for her favorite milkshake or to enjoy the amusements.

Once, while riding her bicycle around the reservation, Becky fell off, skinning her arms, knees and shoulders enough to require attention at Virginia Beach Hospital but they decided not to worry her Mother with news about that. She also spent most of two days at the cottage of the Edward E. Lanes, close friends.

The Grady Norfleets were to come down from Chuckatuck for the weekend and Becky asked that they bring "Muff", their jointly-owned cat. Weekend visitors included the Shirley T. Hollands from Windsor and Mrs. Godwin's foster parents, Mr. and Mrs. Emory Beale. A. Gordon Brooks and his wife Polly, old friends from Chuckatuck days, were to arrive on Monday to stay for a week while the Governor was away.

Mrs. Godwin and her nurse, Miss Margaret Kauffman, moved in as soon as the patient was released at the hospital.

The cottage was becoming a bit crowded and to her delight Becky was moved into her Daddy's room to occupy the other twin bed. It was something of a last gesture to childhood.

She was, in Mrs. Godwin's words, "beginning to blossom. Her big adjustment was over. Of course, her life had been harder than if she had reveled in a life that some children might have liked.

"Our little girl had grown up—not completely, not without her problems to face but almost overnight in the late spring and early summer she had come from a child to a young lady with anticipation of completing school at St. Catherines and looking forward to attending college, hopefully at William and Mary, for she loved Williamsburg.

"She even had planned how she could get home from school on weekends during the year after we left the Mansion. She had talked with her Daddy, too, about spending some time in Europe.

"She had begun to place her values. Mrs. (Edward) Lane and others had noticed that and commented on it".

This was the memory they were to have of her.

Rising before 6 a.m. to have an early breakfast an enplane for Chicago, the Governor did not disturb the sleeping Becky but kissed her and tip-toed from the room.

Assured that Mrs. Godwin was in competent hands and well on the road to complete recovery, he left for the Richmond Airport where the plane of Lloyd U. Noland, a long-time friend from Newport News, was waiting to speed the party on its way.

Accompanying him were his right hand man, Carter O. Lowance; his Suffolk law partner, Sam Glasscock; Sen. Edward L. Breeden of Norfolk and Officer R. W. Shields of the State Police.

127

Most of the Virginia delegation had reached Chicago on Saturday, August 24, and was eagerly awaiting the arrival of Governor Godwin Sunday afternoon but there was no time for a get-together.

As the State's favorite son candidate—something all knew to be hopeless from the start—it was his task to hold the faction-ridden delegation together and try to work out an accommodation with other Southern States to put a conservative or a least a moderate on the ticket with Humphrey. Most seemed to favor former Gov. John Connally of Texas.

Godwin left his own hotel almost immediately to go to the Palmer House for the Southern strategy session and returned anything but optimistic.

Moscoe Garnett, Suffolk chairman for the impending bond campaign, was waiting to discuss plans. Present also was Sidney Kellam of Virginia Beach, former national committeeman and a powerful figure in the Democratic Organization for years, as well as Carter Lowance and Officer Shields.

They had been in the room only a short time when a message came that there was an emergency call for Lowance in the suite of Garland Harwood, delegation secretary.

Godwin later said that he felt this was most unusual and that he had "a premonition of bad news".

Lowance returned in a matter of minutes and, recalls the Governor, "he was ashen gray and shaken. I knew something had happened".

Lowance asked him to step into the adjoining room.

"Is it Katherine?" he asked, fearing to utter the words.

"No, it's Becky!"

Struggling to control his own emotions, Lowance then explained that the call was from Virginia Beach police who advised that Becky had been killed by lightning.

The awesome news sent Godwin's senses reeling, stunned and overwhelmed.

"I simply couldn't believe it", he said later in recounting events of the terrible day.

Not trusting his own emotions, the Governor asked Lowance to call the cottage at Camp Pendleton direct and find out what had happened.

It developed that the news had reached the Governor almost at the moment it was being broken to Mrs. Godwin in the presence of her nurse, Miss Kauffman.

The telephone was answered by Lucille Anderson, the Mansion cook, who provided some measure of relief when she said that Becky was not dead but had been badly hurt and was in the hospital.

It developed that Becky had been swimming in the surf with Grady Norfleet not far from the cottage. A number of National Guardsmen and their families were enjoying the water also.

There had been some thunder and lightning from an approaching storm but nothing severe. Nevertheless, Becky suggested they leave the beach and Norfleet agreed.

They had just emerged from the water when a bolt struck, knocking down both girl and companion. Norfleet was rendered unconscious. Nearby Guardsmen and State Policeman S. F. Bennett gave the child mouth-to-mouth resuscitation and an ambulance was called from the caretaker's cottage, located near the Governor's cottage. Mrs. Godwin heard the thunderclap and the ambulance which came quickly.

Oxygen was given Becky in the ambulance but she was turning blue when the hospital was reached. There other artificial respiration methods restored breathing.

Meanwhile Norfleet was revived and somehow made his way to the cottage, covered with sand. He even talked to Lowance on the telephone although never being able to remember it. Later he was taken to the hospital, much against his will, and remained several days recuperating.

Back in Chicago, Kellam suggested that the physician on duty at the Virginia Beach Hospital probably was Dr. Richard Robertson, who had married his niece.

He and Lowance then called the hospital and talked with Dr. Robertson twice, learning that while Becky was alive, her chances for survival were minimal.

The hospital asked for permission to perform a tracheotomy to insert a tube and assist the breathing process. This was permitted immediately.

What little interest Godwin had in the convention now was at an end and he informed key members of the delegation that he was leaving as quickly as possible.

Lowance managed reservations on a commercial flight to Washington where they were to be met by the State plane and flown to Norfolk.

The first inkling the large Virginia press delegation had of the tragedy was when the Governor, Lowance and the rest of the party emerged from the elevator in the lobby and Godwin broke the news. They had not even unpacked.

There was an agonizing delay at Washington National Airport as the plane was kept circling by a violent thunderstorm. Finally they got down and rushed to the State plane where Maj. Kenneth A. Rowe, assistant director of the Division of Aeronautics and his copilot were waiting. The flight to Norfolk seemed almost interminable but by midnight the Governor was standing by the bedside of the little girl he had kissed goodby in her sleep only 18 hours before.

The medical staff headed by Dr. Robertson was doing everything humanly possible to save her life and she was fighting valiantly but Godwin realized that her life was hanging by a thin thread.

While swimming, Becky had swept her hair back and held it in place with a metal clip. Examinations later showed that the lightning struck this, went through her brain, lungs and body, causing kidney malfunction and eventually cardiac arrest.

At the hospital he saw Mrs. Norfleet and heard for the first time that his hometown neighbor was injured and under treatment.

After talking with Dr. Robertson, he hastened to Camp Pendleton to see Mrs. Godwin and try to comfort her, leaving family and friends to maintain the vigil.

His two sisters were on hand as were Judge James C. Godwin, his minister, Dr. Millard Stevens from Chuckatuck, and the Edward Lanes.

At the cottage there was a large group of friends including

130

the Shirley Hollands, his staff, state troopers and their longtime close personal friends, Dr. and Mrs. Richard B. Nicholls of Norfolk, as well as the nurse. Dr. Nicholls had performed the operation on Mrs. Godwin.

Back he went to the hospital, seeking desperately to help the child rally by calling her name but there was no sign of recognition. Then back to the cottage where he and Lowance spent a sleepless night, getting occasional telephoned bulletins.

Monday morning President and Mrs. Johnson called from the White House to express sympathy. Vice President Humphrey tried unsuccessfully to get through from Chicago. At an early hour Lowance met with the press to give them the first complete story.

A Good Listener.

There followed days of vigil with Godwin at the hospital morning, afternoon and far into the night. Once, on Tuesday, Becky showed signs of regaining consciousness. Her eyes opened and seemed to focus on her father but she could not speak and there was no sign of recognition.

Dr. Robley D. Bates, personal friend and physician, flew down twice from Richmond to assist in diagnosis. Kidney specialists from the Medical College of Virginia in Richmond and the University of Virginia Medical School at Charlottesville likewise flew in.

Thursday morning the doctors insisted that he return to Camp Pendleton. They did not have to tell him that the end was near. ·

One last desperate effort remained to be made. Call was made for special respirator machine at the University of Virginia. Col. Harold W. Burgess, head of the State Police, arranged a special escort and it was sent speeding across the state. It was too late and probably would have made no difference.

When Dr. Robertson arrived at Camp Pendleton shortly before 2 p.m. on the afternoon of August 29, the Governor knew it was all over.

Their only solace was in knowing that had she lived she would not have been normal ever again physically or mentally. This, they could not, in all conscience hope or pray for.

Looking back upon that soul-shaking period of grief which was to vanquish the happiness they had known in the Governor's Mansion, Godwin spoke of how they were sustained only by their deep faith in God, a sentiment she echoed:

"Katherine and I both tried to accept Becky's passing—it was not easy to give her up—we could not understand—we hardly could begin to understand the meaning of it all—we faced up to what we had to face—Mrs. Godwin was exceedingly brave —I tried to be—I had to be for obvious reasons".

Even in their grief, he found time to thank the doctors and nurses who bore the brunt of the unsuccessful fight for life.

They decided that the funeral should be Saturday, August 31, from the Mansion in Richmond with burial in the family plot in Holly Lawn Cemetery in Suffolk. Lowance took over and made all arrangements.

At the Capitol and over all state buildings flags came to half mast. In Chicago the sad news was announced by Chairman Carl Albert of Oklahoma and the great Democratic convention stood in silent tribute.

More than 10,000 messages of condolence poured in from all over the State and Nation, many of them from people the Godwins did not know personally. By the funeral hour floral

132

tributes were overflowing the Mansion, whose first floor had been stripped of furniture to accommodate much of the thousands who came and even filled the yard.

Included among the mourners were three governors: Dan. K. Moore of North Carolina, Robert E. McNair of South Carolina and Huelett C. Smith of West Virginia with their wives together with a vast array of former governors of Virginia, members of Congress, members of the General Assembly, government officials, judges and people from all walks of life. Many of them had known Becky personally.

The family's two pastors, W. Millard Stevens from Oakland Christian in Chuckatuck and Richard A. Cheek of St. John's Christian in Richmond, conducted the brief but moving services at the Mansion and again at the Suffolk cemetery where another huge throng awaited.

Classmates from St. Catherines had a special place at the services for the little girl they had learned to love because she was herself and not just the Governor's daughter.

A room in the new library at St. Catherines will be a permanent memorial and a trust has been established there for the annual purchase of books for the library in Becky's memory.

A scholarship fund was established by the Virginia Education Association. Thousands of dollars were given to life saving crews in all parts of the state, especially at Virginia Beach. Jewish friends raised a fund to plant trees in her memory in Israel where reforestation is planned to restore beauty of Biblical days. Editorials of sympathy appeared in hundreds of newspapers of Virginia and around the Nation. Services of four secretaries were required for many days to acknowledge messages.

In years to come visitors to the Mansion's lovely garden will be reminded of a little girl who once played there because friends have planted a "Cherokee Princess" dogwood tree in her memory with a little bronze plaque bearing the name of Becky.

Only those who have lost a child can understand fully the adjustment which now had to be made by Katherine and Mills Godwin, she still under the care of her nurse while continuing to recuperate and therefore unable to throw herself into the task of running the Mansion.

For a week the Governor hardly left her side or went out-

133

side the Mansion. But then he realized that he must get back to the helm of Virginia's ship of state. In addition, only 60 days remained before the historic $81 million bond referendum which he had demanded to help speed Old Dominion progress.

One week after the funeral he had been scheduled to speak at the dedication of a new wing of a hospital in Newport News. Mrs. Lewis A. McMurran, Jr., wife of one of the Democratic leaders in the House of Delegates, was chairman. He found it the most difficult public appearence he had ever made but, he confessed later, "it helped me get a new start on life".

Two weeks later he had speeches scheduled on successive days—on bonds at King William High School and to dedicate the new King George High School. Tempted to shuck the whole thing, he finally decided that he must keep occupied.

From then on he threw himself into the bond campaign with more than usual vigor, sometimes speaking two and three times a day, with the highlight a statewide rally of the Virginia Federation of Women's Clubs attended by over a thousand women at Hotel John Marshall.

Like so many others before him, Mills Godwin found healing for grief in hard work. It was really the only thing which sustained him that year in the great old Mansion, once so desirable but now so strangely empty.

THE PEOPLE ABANDON PAY-AS-YOU-GO

Nothing better illustrates the change which can be wrought in voter thinking in a short period of 15 years than what happened between the defeat of Ted Dalton for Governor in 1953 and the successful referendum on $81 million in State bonds in 1968.

134

Bond Salesman: Godwin proved by far most effective spokesman for the $81 million bond issue for colleges and hospitals. Here the photographer caught him driving home points.

In 1953 Republican Dalton generally was conceded the edge over Thomas B. Stanley until he proposed late in the campaign a $100 million bond issue for highway construction. As has been noted, that brought the aging Sen. Harry Byrd into the campaign with both feet and Stanley won.

In 1968 it was a different story, as we shall see. Governor Godwin, the master politician with a superb sense of timing and a remarkable ability to interpret as well as to lead public thinking, had covered every part of the state repeatedly for seven years.

"I sensed that the people of Virginia were anxious to get the State moving. Everywhere I went they told me they wanted to do what needed doing", he said. "Their acceptance of the sales tax had proved their willingness and determination".

The bond act had passed the General Assembly and was signed by Godwin on February 9 before the session was half over. If approved by the electorate on November 5, it would make $67.2 million available for construction at institutions of higher learning and $13.77 million for similar work at the mental hospitals.

The job was to "sell" the people on the necessity. He knew that he had alienated the old line die-hard Byrd followers as he had earned the enmity of the Massive Resisters in 1965. In addition, substantial numbers of Republicans were opposed, as their spokesmen had indicated in the General Assembly.

It was obvious that the campaign must be absolutely nonpartisan if the bonds were to be approved because the referendum would be held simultaneous with the presidential-congressional election.

Thus it was that on May 16 Godwin announced his intention to concentrate on the bonds and avoid politics because, he explained later, "I wanted and had to have the support of Republicans as well as Democrats".

It was not a particularly hard decision to make. Although he later was to go to the Democratic National Convention in Chicago as Virginia's favorite son and as a possible rallying figure for the South, he anticipated the nomination of Vice President Humphrey, for whom he had no great admiration, and had pledged that he would support the nominee of the convention.

That was it. He never spoke for the Humphrey-Muskie ticket because "I could not speak one night for the bonds and the next for the Democratic ticket and expect bipartisan support of the bonds. I think it was a very wise decision".

Godwin built his organization with great care. On May 28 he called former State Sen. Leonard G. Muse of Roanoke whom he considered to be "probably one of the best informed men about educational needs of the state on every level" and asked him to act as chairman.

Muse, who accepted after recovering from his surprise, had served 12 years in the Senate as a key man in the Education Committee, 22 years on the State Board of Education (1941-63) the last three as chairman, had served on the Roanoke City School Board and currently was Rector of the Board of Visitors at Radford College and Vice President of the Board of Trustees at Roanoke College. A senior partner in the law firm of Woods, Rogers, Muse, Walker and Thornton, he had also served as chairman of the Governor's regional Conference on Education in 1966 at Roanoke, one of the most successful of that series of rallies.

Godwin also called on William H. Trapnell, president of the Commonwealth National Gas Corp., to lead in raising a

136

$100,000 fund to finance the campaign. Trapnell and his group did so well that the goal was oversubscribed and following the referendum there was a sizeable sum to contribute to the Virginia Foundation for Independent Colleges.

"It was a magnificent effort", appraised the Governor.

Let Muse pick up the story:

"I was impressed with two things especially—Governor Godwin's ability to get people of varying views to work together and his determination and that of other leaders to keep the bond sales effort (we decided not to call it a campaign because that sounded too political) nonpartisan, in fact non-everything except the welfare of Virginia.

"There were no political overtones and we were careful to avoid calling on any partisans for help.

"The Governor promised to go any place any time he could fit it into his schedule. We met possibly a half dozen times. I had to confess my lack of acquaintance with leaders in every part of the State and asked him for help. He provided me with a list of people that covered Virginia like a blanket.

"I called each one of these by telephone and explained that I was doing so at the suggestion of the Governor and, do you know, not a single one said 'no'!

"These included people who were interested in both schools and the mental hospitals. The Governor was so earnest that they wanted to help".

There was no steering committee but occasionally Muse met with the Governor and his staff including Carter Lowance, John Wessells and Mrs. Pat Perkinson. They maintained an office in old Hotel Richmond with Dick Taylor, young Richmond Lawyer, as coordinator, and a staff of three young women.

The summer was spent getting geared up for the big effort with nothing left to chance because, Godwin reminisced later, "passage was absolutely necessary—it would have taken this State ten years to recover from its defeat".

As matters turned out, the people had great confidence in Godwin and trusted his appraisal of Virginia's situation.

On January 20 he had promised at Norfolk: "While I hold this office, Virginia will borrow money only to meet critical needs, only with a specific limitation, only with an iron-clad guarantee of

137

repayment and only with the approval of the people themselves".

On February 4 in a press conference he posed the question simply: "The issue is which way this State will move". And again to a Richmond audience: "The issue is not deficit financing but deficit education".

Twice in April, first to Virginia School Superintendents at Roanoke and again to an assemblage at the famed Wakefield Shad Planking of Sen. Garland Gray in the woods of Sussex County, he set the pattern for the bond drive.

Potential Republican opposition was dealt a sharp blow when the party's No. 1 man, Linwood Holton, pledged to vote "aye". GOP House Leader M. Caldwell Butler spoke out favorably. So did Sen. H. D. "Buzz" Dawbarn of Waynesboro.

All candidates for the Democratic gubernatorial nomination —Lt. Gov. Fred Pollard, Sen. Henry E. Howell, Jr. and William C. Battle—spoke out vigorously. So did Dr. T. Marshall Hahn, VPI president, who never got around to announcing but had been a strong advocate from the start. Howell urged Virginians to be "evangelical" in the cause. Sen. William B. Hopkins, of Roanoke, soon to be chosen Democratic national committeeman, warned that the only alternative to bonds was tax increases.

Dr. Hiram W. Davis, commissioner of the State Department of Hygiene and Hospitals, members of his board and leaders in the Mental Health Association took the lead for hospital bonds. It was a credit to them that in the end voters gave their proposition the biggest majority.

The State press was practically unanimous in its editorial backing for both issues and was later credited by both Godwin and Muse with playing a most influential role.

One of the most telling efforts was made by presidents of the institutions of higher learning who addressed letters to every state resident alumnus, reciting the individual needs of their alma maters.

There were only two alarming aspects. Public meetings in all parts of the State were sparsely attended except for speeches by the Governor. And a body of conservatives with spokesmen like Robert T. Marsh, Jr., retired Richmond banker, led opposition which largely resorted to advertising in newspapers. Two months before the referendum a survey by the Virginia Farm

Bureau News showed 83 per cent of its rural readers ready to vote "no".

Stunned for a time by the tragic loss of his daughter, Becky, Godwin threw himself with renewed determination into the last six weeks of the effort with the warning that "by ignoring the needs today we are only compounding the problem for future generations".

At last the battle was over and on the eve of the referendum Governor Godwin and his staff had time to look at one another in exhausted manner as they tried to guess what might happen.

For Godwin especially it was the moment of truth for if the people rejected the bonds and decided to stick with what was good enough for their fathers his four-year program, begun so auspiciously, would be brought to a grinding halt.

Giving way to that famous grin and trying to ease the staff's own tension, he observed wryly: "If we lose this thing, I will feel like Hurricane Branch who ran for sheriff down our way. He went all around the county talking to everybody and was really sure that he had overwhelming support, but when the votes were counted, he had miserably few and he lost the race. Somebody asked him why he lost. 'Well', he said, 'there sure are a lot of liars!' ".

It was a far different picture the next night as the results poured in showing the bonds had carried by impressive 2 to 1 margins with not over a half dozen political units rejecting.

Surprisingly the hospital bonds received the biggest vote, in round figures 785,000 to 323,000 while the college capital bonds went over 773,000 to 390,000.

"The result never really was in doubt", observed Muse, "but the margin of success was much bigger than any of us had dared hope. I would have settled for a 10,000 vote margin statewide. But the people understood the need and they were ready and willing to go ahead".

Nobody could blame Godwin for being elated.

"It was truly a test of how deep and how strong runs the current of support for education in Virginia", he summarized although confessing that the vote—in effect a decision to scrap pay-as-you-go—"did not come easy to many of those who supported it".

139

There was quick tribute for Senator Muse's leadership: "It was a great job. I shall always be grateful to him. It was truly a remarkable effort. It was the finest organized and best executed of any campaign for any public issue in many years in Virginia".

Pressed for an assessment of his part, he added modestly: "If I have done anything well as Governor of Virginia it was the pleasing success of this bond referendum".

"It was", he added, "a politician's dream".

The fact that the Democratic national ticket of Humphrey and Muskie ran a poor second to Nixon and Agnew and might have been even further behind had not George Wallace been in the race, caused Governor Godwin little grief. It was no surprise and, in his opinion, "they never had a chance".

He remembered calling on Humphrey in Washington with other Southern governors in July shortly after the National Governors conference in Cincinnati.

"We advised him that he could not hope to carry the South unless he chose a running mate who was interested in this area. He listened but showed no interest in following the advice. In fact, he refused to do so and chose Muskie".

Nixon, he added, "would have won by a substantial majority in Virginia had not Wallace been on the ballot. The Humphrey vote would have been the same had Wallace not been a candidate".

Regardless of that, the bond referendum result marked the high tide for the Godwin vote-getting magic—a magic he was unable to transfer to a Democratic candidate who tried to be his successor a year later.

REALIZING A JEFFERSONIAN DREAM

Dedicating the new North Campus of Roanoke's Virginia Western Community College, Oct. 28, 1969, Godwin gets rapt attention from members of Community Colleges Board.

Given its impetus by the 1966 General Assembly, the State Board for Community Colleges set out to achieve fruition for one of the fondest dreams of Thomas Jefferson—bringing education to the people.

Community colleges were nothing new, of course. Excellent systems in California and Florida were serving as a challenge to other states. The Virginia State Board of Education had given serious thought to a system of two-year junior colleges to help take the burden off four-year colleges and to reach thousands of

141

youths whose families lacked the means to send them away to complete their educations.

As we have noted, established institutions began meeting some of the need, first through extension classes then in building branches to give the equivalent of the first two years of college. VPI in particular did an excellent job in setting up vocational-technical branches.

It was becoming generally recognized that not every high school graduate needs or can benefit by a college degree.

Dr. Dana B. Hamel had scarcely started his task as director when he predicted on June 1, 1966, that the system would have an enrollment of between 25,000 and 30,000 within two years. He was a fairly accurate prophet for September 1968 saw 22,797 students matriculated at 13 community colleges.

Virginia Western at Roanoke, a consolidation of VPI's technical branch and the U. Va. extension school, became first to open and has remained the largest. Altogether that first fall the system had two community colleges and five area vocational-technical schools in operation for 7,573 students.

The next year found two of the vo-tech schools transformed, with 11 institutions serving 12,370.

The Board's master plan, projecting 23 colleges in 22 areas or districts by September 1, 1971, had been completed by a firm of consultant experts in January, 1967, and $27 million already had been spent in state and federal funds on operation and capital development.

Passage of the $81 million bond issue in November, 1968, provided a tremendous boost of $5.58 million and guaranteed that the system could be completed on time. Within three weeks sites for the remaining 10 schools had been designated.

September, 1969, saw 13 colleges functioning and serving 28,955 students. So well was the job being done that five institutions had been accredited by the Southern Association of Colleges and Schools on December 1—no mean achievement because that body does not distribute its blessings indiscriminately.

Barely three years old as this is written, the Virginia Community College system already has become a national model and the object of study by governmental and educational officials from other states.

What is the secret of success?

Probably the fact that no two are alike. Each college is organized with the specific needs of the people of its service district in mind. Each region has a minimum population of 100,000 and the school is within 45 minutes driving time of every student.

Organized on the quarter system, they are open the year around, six days a week. That is near-maximum utilization.

Anyone can enroll if he has a high school diploma or its equivalent or is 18 and can show through counseling or tests that he can benefit from the programs.

It is a source of satisfaction to Governor Godwin and every legislator who supported the program that 98 per cent of students in the system are Virginia residents.

Possibly even more pleasing is that out of 1,184 to graduate in 1969, 82 per cent were in occupational-technical fields and of these 92 per cent have been employed in Virginia. The money spent on their education was a wise investment. All are now taxpayers and some started at salaries ranging up to $11,000.

As the State's super salesman to industry, Godwin has been especially elated over the contribution of the Special Training Division of the Community Colleges. Working with industry, the Division set up training programs to equip over 12,000 people for job holding in 82 new or expanded industries between 1966 and 1969, over 50 per cent of them previously unemployed or not in the labor market. The cost of training: $94 per person. Each one now returns far more than that in income and sales tax each year.

The mere establishment of a community college in any area, points out Dr. Hamel, is the equivalent of setting up a medium sized industry. In addition to payrolls, in some cases over $1 million a year, the students and their families contribute greatly.

In other words, the new system is living up to its boast of being "where the future is built today".

Appropriately enough, Godwin could say in addressing the National Council of State Directors of Community Colleges at Williamsburg:

"The phenomenal growth of the two-year college across the nation is in accord with Jefferson's belief that freedom cannot survive in the midst of ignorance, and that higher education, therefore, cannot be only for those who were born to it or who can afford it".

Again, in dedicating the new North Campus of Virginia Western at Roanoke on Oct. 23, 1969, he recalled Jefferson's writing of a personal epitaph:

"I am not ready to write my epitaph quite yet, but if I were, the small part I have played in bringing Virginia's Community College system into being would surely be my first choice".

That, he said, would offset being remembered as the man who brought the sales tax to Virginia and sold it on the idea of issuing general obligation bonds to meet its needs.

Perhaps he summed it all up best with a declaration that in three years the system had become "a working monument to the working people of this Commonwealth".

The greatest foe of a continuing successful community college system, as Godwin sees it, is the alarming trend especially evidenced by Republican candidates in the 1969 election campaign to advocate "chipping away" by converting the two-year schools into four-year colleges in urban areas.

—Roanoke Times and World-News Photo

First Community College in the new system to open, Virginia Western at Roanoke more than doubled its facilities with a new campus (top) dedicated by Governor Godwin Oct. 28, 1969.

144

Such a thing, he believes, would be a serious mistake when the State already is supporting 14 four-year institutions.

Sen. Leonard G. Muse, of Roanoke, who led the 1968 bond campaign and who is described by the Governor as one of the State's most knowledgeable men in education, agrees that the conversion would be "tragic". Technical and vocational education would suffer, he says, and the primary purpose would be lost. Further, it is difficult enough for the established four-year institutions to obtain and keep qualified faculties without having more competition. Worst of all would be the additional splitting of available tax dollars for higher education.

Obviously, not all Virginians and far from all politicians have caught the vision of community college purpose. Keeping the system intact is going to require vigilance and dedication.

Yet, this was only one facet of a remarkable overall plan designed and put in operation by Godwin in a four-year period to pull his State educationally into the Twentieth Century.

Total appropriations for capital outlays for institutions of higher learning ($163,841,830) exceeded the expenditures for 20 previous years by $10.5 million. As a result, enrollments could shoot up from 55,000 to 96,000 and graduate programs were strengthened in astonishing fashion.

With the worst of the long, bitter and enervating racial integration fight now over, Godwin was determined to elevate the standards of public schools. And, as we have seen, enactment of the sales tax, enabling the state to do its share and virtually to compel reciprocal action on the local level, has accomplished the task in main.

Between 1965-66 and 1969-70 State aid to localities jumped from $167 million to $355 million and total expenditures in this field from $514 million to $769 million.

The minimum teacher salary scale ascended from $3,700—$5,000 to $5,000—$6,800. The classroom teacher average went from $5,725 to $7,850. In 1965 only 89 per cent of teachers held degrees. By 1970 the figure was 93 per cent and rising fast.

For the first time the State put up money to help local systems finance summer schools. In 1968 a $15 million outlay helped launch the kindergarten program. Educational television is subsidized in a small way. Help has been given in textbook

145

rental systems as well as free text books and new emphasis was put on vocational training in realization that not all boys and girls are destined to be scholars.

It is almost superfluous to say that because of these achievements Governor Godwin had become the idol of educators of Virginia long before his term ended.

Let three of them speak for all.

Undoubtedly one of the closest to Godwin of all institutional presidents has been Dr. T. Marshall Hahn of Virginia Polytechnic Institute, who the Governor named to head the far-reaching study on local government, who nearly ran for the honor of succeeding him and without whose energetic support the Community College system might not have been realized.

"Mills Godwin takes with him a record of accomplishment unequalled in Virginia's modern history. No more able governor has appeared in this century . . . Fortuitous accident of time and place undoubtedly played a part in the political maturity of his administration. But in less skilled and resolute hands no such record of achievement could have been made possible . . . That he has been so successful testifies eloquently to his leadership ability. But it also indicates his ability to adapt genuinely conservative convictions to the changing needs of the Commonwealth . . . regardless of who leads Virginia in the decades ahead, the legacy of the Godwin years will remain—his personal and political influence is reflected in almost every aspect of State government".

Discussing the accomplishments, Dr. Hahn cited prominently "Creation of a statewide community college system over the determined opposition of some political and educational leaders who appeared to place local and institutional considerations in higher priority than the State's educational needs. The compromise and political contortion attending the birth of the community college system very nearly resulted in its legislative death even before its first breath. . ."

"The extent of Governor Godwin's enthusiastic efforts toward strengthening of higher education perhaps is not as well recognized at it should be", he added, praising, among other things, upgrading of faculty salaries, meeting greater capital needs, and expanding the scope of college education. And, in summary:

"The renewed commitment to public higher education, and the determination to adapt it better to Virginia's educational needs in a changing economy, ultimately may be the greatest single accomplishment of the Godwin years".

Hear Dr. Edgar F. Shannon, president of the University of Virginia:

"Governor Godwin made the advance of education the major concern of his administration; then, with great skill and energy he developed the public support that permitted him to convert his concerns into laws and appropriations. . . In his very first year in office he did more to advance the cause of public education than any governor in living memory. . .

"His enthusiasm, his frank admission of Virginia's educational backwardness, and his unflagging hard work were all vital factors in his success in overcoming the apathy that had retarded public education in his State. He has never spared himself in teaching his fellow citizens to recognize our shortcomings and needs. The resulting accomplishments for education are unparalleled in modern Virginia history".

Finally, there is this appraisal from Dr. Davis Y. Paschall, president of the College of William and Mary and former State Superintendent of Public Instruction:

"Governor Godwin evidenced a most enlightened leadership throughout his administration. The achievements in all areas of public service have been so profound as to warrant history's according him a role of twentieth century statesman comparable in so many ways to that of Jefferson in former times. His advocacy and support of education at all levels have brought "full circle" the dream of Jefferson in the diffusion of knowledge throughout this Commonwealth.

"He gave of himself so devotedly and sacrificially that his spirit infused members of the General Assembly and people in all walks of life in support of his endeavors. This is evidenced in the great strides made in kindergartens, elementary and secondary schools, in the development of community colleges, and in the tremendous support given the institutions of higher learning. His advocacy of constitutional revision, and change with stability in so many spheres—all constitute a thrilling challenge to those who would, in future years, do well to emulate his exemplary leadership".

Thomas Jefferson, a product of William and Mary, realized in his lifetime the accomplishment of one part of his dream when his beloved University of Virginia was built and opened as the capstone of an ideal system of education. But his vision of State-supported schools within the reach of all was denied.

It remained for Mills E. Godwin, Jr., a product of both of Jefferson's favored institutions, to lead the way in giving more substance to the dream. Assuredly his upgrading of the public schools, establishment of a community college system and emphasis on improving the four-year colleges and universities had brought the dream closer to reality.

It is something for which to be remembered.

ALL IS NOT ROSES

Governors, like other mortals, would rather remember only the good things of their administrations and trust that time mercifully will shroud the bad, making trials and tribulations which once seemed so great mere incidents along the way.

There are things which Mills Godwin wishes devoutly had never happened but he is proud that he did not shrink from the decisions which had to be made.

Foremost among the unpleasant memories is the furor in the summer of 1967 which compelled him to remove a lifelong friend, R. Stanley Holland, from the State Highway Commission.

148

Mr. Holland, representative of the Suffolk District but a resident of Virginia Beach, had been disclosed in newspaper stories as involved in ownership of land corporations which sold property to contractors for gravel pits and fill material used in highway construction.

There were accusations that he was responsible for leaking word of highway routings, particularly of the Norfolk-Virginia Beach Expressway, to friends and associates who profited thereby. Politicians, mainly from the Democratic liberal wing and Republicans, were joined in criticism by newspaper editorials demanding his removal.

Unable to ignore the situation, Governor Godwin ordered a special investigation by Virginius Shackelford, of Orange, a former Virginia State Bar president.

After a lengthy probe, Shackelford reported to the Governor that he found no evidence of law violation or wrong-doing but criticised Holland as being guilty of poor judgment.

Holland apparently considered this sufficient vindication but, with the 1967 legislative election campaign getting under way and with public criticism not the least allayed, Godwin felt compelled to act.

He called Holland to his office and, reminding him that public officials must be above suspicion like Caesar's wife, suggested rather gently, he thought, that Holland "might want to consider resigning". Recalls the Governor:

"Much to my surprise, he reacted rather strongly. His position was that he had done nothing wrong, that there was no evidence that he had done anything wrong, that there were only some suspicions and that these were unfounded—that they had been made by political enemies, his own and liberals of the Democratic Party, by persons not friendly to me as Governor or to the Organization, as well as by Republicans".

Holland did not resign. Godwin called him in again and gave him a week to make up his mind. At the same time the Governor contacted mutual friends and enlisted their aid in urging resignation.

Nothing happened and finally "despite our friendship, I had to act", says Godwin. With great regret, he wrote a letter which he dispatched by State Trooper for personal delivery notifying

149

Holland of his removal from the commission.

Adds the Governor, wincing even now at the thought:

"It was a painful decision for me to make but I felt there was no alternative. I did not shrink from what I thought was my responsibility and duty. I was not unaware that this might break a friendship of long standing. To this day it has not been mended —much to my regret. I wish very much it was otherwise".

It was the first time in modern State history that such a thing had been done. To fill the vacancy, he chose W. Fred Duckworth, former mayor of Norfolk and a leading businessman.

On another occasion, Godwin demanded and received the resignation of a member of a State board whose personal affairs had become involved to the point of scandal but there never was any necessity for publicity.

Most of the Governor's other headaches involved preservation of law and order. In the same summer as the Holland affair (1967) a wildcat strike of some 1,000 to 1,500 employes of the Newport News Shipbuilding and Dry Dock Co. erupted into sudden violence with window smashing and much property damage along public streets.

At the request of Mayor Don Hyatt, Godwin rushed in 125 State Troopers, steel-helmeted and fully equipped to suppress rioting. They quickly restored and maintained order.

Asked to mediate, Godwin agreed on one condition: that spokesmen for both management and union (the Peninsula Shipbuilders Association) meet in his office and that all pickets be withdrawn while negotiations were under way.

This was done and he talked with both sides until 3 o'clock in the morning. They resumed the next day and finally secured an agreement by late that afternoon.

Godwin had reason to be proud of the way State Police together with Newport News police had handled the crisis and of the manner in which peace was brought to the shipbuilding city.

1967 seems to have been Godwin's year of crises. Speaking to the Planters Club in Suffolk one evening in May, he had a note passed to him by a member of the press, telling of the assassination of Dr. Martin Luther King in Memphis. He informed the crowd and expressed the hope that civil disorders would not follow although fearing the consequences. While driving back to

150

Richmond, he kept the radio on all the way, listening to the flood of news.

The next morning he was the recipient of many many calls from Negroes urging that the Virginia State flag be lowered to halfmast. To each he explained that this would not be done unless the President had ordered the Flag of the United States halfmasted.

As soon as word came of President Johnson's order to that effect, he complied and lowered the Virginia flag also. To leave one full mast and the other half-raised would have been an unusual situation, to say the least. But, he again was deluged with calls, this time from right-wingers, "giving me the devil".

Negroes asked for permission to use the Capitol south portico for a Sunday memorial service and this being within proper policy "because the Capitol belongs to all the people", he complied, but again over protests of militant whites. The rally was held peacefully with about 600 attending while the Governor and his family spent the weekend in Williamsburg.

Friday night meanwhile disorder broke out in Richmond with large gangs of young blacks roaming the streets, damaging automobiles, breaking windows, starting fires and turning in false alarms.

Godwin immediately ordered in 225 State Troopers to supplement Richmond police and nip the trouble in the bud. He did not want to use the National Guard as so many other governors did. There were disorders in other cities, notably Petersburg and Suffolk with large black population, but nothing serious. By showing a firm hand and encouraging local authorities to do the same, he avoided what became a bad situation elsewhere.

There was a corollary later when Gov. Lurleen Wallace of Alabama died and immediately segregationists and rightists demanded "equal treatment" for her memory with that of King. Two or three southern states went along, but Godwin stuck to what he pointed out was Virginia policy. President Johnson did not order half-masting and neither did Godwin. The white anger soon subsided.

More trouble threatened when H. Rap Brown, a loud-mouthed black radical, got into trouble at Cambridge, Maryland, being accused of inciting riot among other things, and fled to

Virginia. He was arrested on the steps of the federal building in Alexandria and a hassle ensued over jurisdiction.

There were fears for his safety due to other extremists so he was rushed to the Richmond city jail for a while and then put in maximum security at the State Farm in Goochland. Later he was bonded and eventually extradited. Outside demonstrators came into Virginia but were kept under close surveillance and trouble was prevented.

Looking back, the Governor salutes the "fine quality of our Negro citizens in Virginia", a vast majority of whom supported law and order just like other citizens. Any one of these incidents could have erupted into trouble but common sense and quick, strong administrative and police action headed it off.

Two other examples of Godwin's firm dealing to calm impending crises are worthy of mention, both of 1969 vintage.

In the Spring of that year a rash of student agitations was sweeping the nation's campuses and apparently a small group at the University of Virginia resolved not to be out of step. They became involved in employe gripes and, making excessive demands, were turned down by Dr. Edgar F. Shannon and the University administration. They then demanded an audience with the Governor which he granted.

The student delegation consisted of three Negroes and four whites, some from out of state. Their written statement made demands including the right of employes to strike and to have collective union bargaining; dismissal of C. Stuart Wheatley of Danville from the board of visitors as a "massive resister" and his replacement with a Negro; more black instructors and immediate institution of more black courses; and active recruiting of black students to attain the State ratio of 20 per cent, regard‧less of qualification but with the state furnishing special tutoring.

Governor Godwin listened patiently and then strongly rejected their demands. First of all, he told them, the Board of Visitors and administration run the University by law, that appointments are not made on the basis of race and that he would not remove Wheatley, a valuable and devoted member.

Wages, he explained, were a matter for the administration and that public employes did not have the right to strike in Virginia, that the University is supported by public funds, that stu-

152

dents were there to get an education and not to run the institution.

Attending Virginia state-operated institutions is a privilege and not a vested right, he added, and closed with an admonition that he would tolerate no disorder there or anywhere else and would use full state power to see that order was maintained.

They shook hands and departed and that was about the end of the incipient rebellion. Godwin wanted "the word" to reach all state colleges and subsequently instructed each administration to be firm and tolerate no disorder.

A flood of mail, telegrams and telephone calls resulted, overwhelmingly in favor of his stand, while the state press backed him editorially.

It was always the Godwin policy to maintain an "open door", so that any citizen who came could be assured of a courteous hearing.

—Richmond Newspapers Photo

How About Letting Us Vote, Governor? A group of 18-year-olds asks Godwin to help get the age limit reduced. From left, Kimberly Winter, Sheila Tucker, Dave Peterson, Brett Vandecastle and Sarah White, acting as spokesman. Tragic loss of daughter deepened his love for youngsters.

This extended to the poor like anyone else and so it was that he listened to a delegation of "Welfare Rights" protesters. A national organization had been formed (by a bunch of do-gooders, in Godwin's opinion) with branches being set up all around the country, "making demands for more money far beyond state resources, staging disorderly demonstrations before local governing bodies and other irritants such as sit-ins at welfare offices".

The chief demand to Godwin was for more money, food, clothing and other concessions. He discovered one was drawing $275 a month and others almost as much while few seemed overly enthusiastic about an old-fashioned word spelled w-o-r-k.

For those who had children in need of food, Godwin arranged for immediate relief by having them fed at the Salvation Army while welfare officials could look into their cases. Only about 40 showed up to take advantage of the offer.

The confrontation calmed what had all the makings of a statewide difficulty which could have been more than just embarrassing. By making it clear that there are no money trees and that the State is doing all it can, working in cooporation with local and federal governments, to combat the burdens of poverty, Godwin ameliorated, if he did not solve, a headache as old as time.

POTPOURRI

There are many lighter moments in the life of a Governor which can help ease the burdens of office with a good laugh.

Take for example what happened one August day in 1966 when Mills Godwin, vacationing at Camp Pendleton, jumped in a jeep alone and, dressed in sport shirt and slacks, drove into Virginia Beach to get a haircut.

154

The lone barber sat in his chair awaiting customers and obviously did not know the Governor, but, in keeping with the reputation of barbers, was full of conversation. He "took off on" the whole U. S. Supreme Court, especially Justice William O. Douglas who, in his seventies, had just wed again, this time to a girl in her twenties. His opinion of no member was very high.

Eventually a portly gentleman entered, took a seat in another chair and began reading, but frequently glancing at Godwin.

"I know who you are!" he soon exclaimed and they shook hands as Godwin prepared to leave.

The barber was a bit stunned.

"Did I understand that you are the Governor?".

Godwin admitted that he was.

"Well, if you don't mind, I wish you would get back in the chair so I can finish cutting your hair", he said. "I hadn't quite finished all I wanted to do to you!"

The finishing, laughs Godwin, took longer than the first session.

But the Governor has a fondness for barbers, in particular "Steve the Barber" (C. H. Stephens) who has operated a shop for lo, these many years, in old Hotel Richmond and still holds his lease in what is now called the Ninth Street State Office Building.

Steve, coming to Richmond from the Kenbridge area of Lunenburg County, has served every governor since Tuck, is a real personality and a no mean forecaster of political events. Business and professional men talk with him as well as legislators and he is a fountain of information.

He has kept governors supplied with toiletries and often remembers girls in the governor's office with perfume. He has been one of Godwin's most vocal supporters.

Then, there is the Godwin penchant for kissing little girls. At the Virginia State Fair in the autumn of 1969 he picked up and kissed a blonde little doll of five or six, unable to resist her beauty. A few days later her father telephoned to say that she had just broken out with chickenpox and he hoped the Governor didn't follow suit. Well, it would have been worth it, the Governor decided.

Not long after that Godwin was visiting the Hugh Mercer

Elementary School in Fredericksburg and, smack, planted a kiss on second grader Jane Payne. Then, remembering the other little girl, he warned that he hoped she wouldn't catch chickenpox from him.

Carl Shires later recorded the next episode in his column in the Richmond News Leader, a letter from Jane addressed to "Dear Mr. Gouvner" which said in part:

"I would have written you sooner but I played a lot with my friends and then after that I went to school and now after all that time has passed I don't have the chickenpox and I wanted you to know I appreciated your kiss and I'm still not sick".

The Governor replied with pleasure in knowing that he was not a carrier.

Speaking of letters, a source of amusement to his staff is the large number of varied salutations. He has been addressed as John Goddin, Governor Gardner, Governor Gorden, Governor Goldwin and most often as Miles Goodwin.

But that does not detract from literally the thousands of letters from people in all walks of life, children and adults, expressing appreciation for his leadership of Virginia in the past four years. They will make interesting volumes in themselves.

Here, Let Me Pin You! Idol of educational circles because of his great school record, Godwin is made an honorary member of the Virginia Congress of Parents and Teachers. Pinning is done by Mrs. W. Hamilton Crockford, III, of the Richmond City School Board.

—Richmond Newspapers Photo

There are, of course, the anonymous, unsigned letters which probably averaged a half dozen per day, received at home and at the office, most with grievances or axes to grind.

As might be expected, some letters contained threats. The height of this came in 1966-67 during the peak of Klan activity, some even being aimed at the Governor's wife and daughter. For weeks the home in Chuckatuck and the farmhouse had to be guarded. Security was increased around the Mansion and additional troopers accompanied him on trips. The FBI got some of the letters.

Aside from this, one of the greatest deluges of mail, telegrams and telephone calls came over "Pokey" the mixed-up whale, who swam up the James River almost to Hopewell one spring day and caused a sensation.

There were countless suggestions for getting him back to the bounding main. But the worst came when an over-ambitious farmer ran a cable around Pokey, lashed him to a tree and tried to end his troubles with a rifle. Long distance calls came from as far away as California and the story was carried nationwide by the press.

"It caused more talk than the sales tax", grins the Governor.

The Governor guessed correctly that people would not object to the sales tax seriously if they could see where their money went. This was impressed on him one day in the summer of 1966 as Trooper Bob Shields was driving the family back to Richmond from Lynchburg. Along the way they halted to let Becky buy an ice cream cone.

While they waited for her and Shields to return to the limousine, a man Godwin had never seen before walked over, identified himself as a Wytheville garage mechanic and said:

"Governor, I want you to know that I appreciate what you have done for young people. You have made possible the Community College in Wytheville where my daughter will enroll a month from now. We never could have afforded to send her to college. We have other children and my income is limited and we never thought we could send any of them beyond high school. But now she can go and we want you to know we appreciate it. I have a feeling that many other people around the State share my gratitude".

Godwin was touched by the deep sincerity.

"This is the sort of thing that keeps public servants happy and rewards them in a way for what they try to do," he says.

There are other things far different which can gratify. Since the 1840's "trusties" from the State Penitentiary have done the yard and garden work around the Mansion, keeping it spotless. They also formerly did heavy cleaning inside the Mansion until Godwin ended the practice.

The Governor always spoke to the trusties, as he would anyone else, with a "good moring" or some other remark.

One day, a strapping big Negro named John Table mustered the courage to speak.

"Governor, suh, I knows who you are. I knew your father and your family. I'm from Longview (a small place about two miles from Chuckatuck) and I have worked on your farm".

Surprised, Godwin pumped for more details. John had killed his wife in a frenzied family affair, had received a 40-year sentence and had by then served 12 years. He asked if the Governor possibly could help him gain his freedom.

Godwin responded that if John would keep out of trouble in the prison until July 4, he would consider urging a parole.

The man had a good record and it was not unnoticed by Godwin that Becky liked him. He frequently would stop work long enough to play basketball with the child.

The upshot was that Godwin arranged a conditional pardon in late 1966 and John went to Ivor to stay with relatives. He had someone telephone the Governor to let him know all was well. A week later he died unexpectedly.

Godwin felt it had all been worthwhile and he was gratified that the man had not had to die in prison.

The satisfaction was equalled only by giving a conditional pardon shortly before leaving office to a former University of Virginia student caught with a large amount of marijuana at Danville and sentenced to 20 years. Feeling that the young man had excellent chances of rehabilitation and had served long enough (nearly a year) he took a chance.

Unfortunately, Godwin did not keep a boxscore on his speeches but he estimates he made over 500 in four years and that doesn't count the impromptu remarks made so often or the

158

airport "whistle stop" talks on bonds during the 1968 campaign.

One of his most unusual public addresses was his 1966 appearance before the AFL-CIO state convention in Roanoke. The organization had backed him for election in 1965 and he had put through increases in both workmen's benefits and unemployment insurance. For the most part, relations with labor continued good. He was the first governor to appear before this group since Colgate Darden in 1942.

As was to be expected, his efforts earned him lasting gratitude of teachers and educators with result that he has been the only governor to speak to four conventions of the Virginia Education Association while in office.

At the last convention on Oct. 31, 1969, Dr. Robert F. Williams, VEA executive director, presented Godwin a scroll designating him as the State's "Education Governor". He also received a handsome piece of Steuben glassware.

He thinks he has done none too much for the 60,000 men and women who teach Virginia's 1,100,000 school children.

Something which perhaps the Governor did not notice but which was not overlooked by staff members who accompanied him was that contrast he furnished with other governors at national and regional meetings. While others played golf or contrived news conferences to promote their political fortunes, Godwin stuck to business and was prepared for the subjects under discussion.

That didn't mean that he always had a speech to make. But when he did speak out his words received wide attention. For example, at Atlanta in 1968 when he was assuming chairmanship of the Southern Regional Education Board.

Gov. Lester Maddox of Georgia had blasted SREB in the press for its report encouraging the upgrading of Negro education. Godwin took the floor to deliver a reply that brought the assemblage to its feet applauding and nationwide editorial commendation followed.

"It was", recalls a staff member with pride, "one of his shining moments".

Where gifts are concerned, the Governor and First Lady received "an unbelieveable number" in their four years at the Mansion, some extremely valuable. Every Governor's Conference yielded dozens, sometimes as many as 50, ranging from shoes and clothing to soap, perfume and books. He estimates eight sport coats alone.

Once the State Chamber of Commerce dressed him in a complete "Made in Virginia" wardrobe, extending from underwear to topcoat and from hat to shoes.

Gifts were so numerous they had to be sent to the home in Chuckatuck for storage. When the new house is ready at Cedar Point Club, it is probable the Godwins will spend many an hour opening what the Governor estimates to be a good-sized truckload. Many gifts have never been out of their original boxes.

Of all the countless trips they made about the State, Godwin probably got more pleasure out of establishing a gubernatorial "first" when he attended finals of the Miss Virginia Pageant at the American Theatre in June, 1969, and crowned Sydney Lee Lewis, the stunning blonde coed from Hampton.

Miss Lewis and many of her predecessors (Godwin has known eight personally) have gone on State Chamber trips to New York and Chicago.

"They have been wonderful sales ladies for Virginia", he summarizes, "and crowning one was a delightful privilege. After all, beautiful girls are one of Virginia's very finest products".

Batter Up! Well, not quite. A lifelong lover of baseball and player in his youth, Godwin tosses first ball from mound rather than box to open the International League season in Richmond. He and daughter Becky were regular rooters.

—Richmond Newspapers Photo

PROMOTING CONSTITUTIONAL CHANGE

Contrary to long-held opinion around the country that Virginia always has enjoyed living in the past and has resisted change as a tribute to its heroes of yesteryear, the State has had seven constitutions since 1776.

The only thing common to all of them has been George Mason's Declaration of Rights which was so magnificent in its conception and wordage that it became the basis of the Bill of Rights to the Federal Constitution on December 15, 1791.

That was and has been the one sacred thing. Just about all else was altered from time to time to meet the needs of the day. The last substantial changes had come when Harry F. Byrd was in the Governor's chair.

When the 1966 General Assembly adjourned after enacting the sales tax and paving the way for passage of the $81 million bond issue in 1968, it was evident to many that constitutional change must follow soon. The tiny Republican minority had advocated a constitutional convention but was ignored.

Erection of the first serious directional signal came on September 13, 1966, when Del. Willis M. Anderson, up-and-coming young legislator, addressed the Roanoke Bar Association, citing the need to abandon pay-as-you-go and biennial sessions along with other major changes. Whether it was done by referendum or convention was immaterial, he said, so long as it was done.

The carefully prepared talk, repeated before the Fairfax Bar Association and other organizations, created a statewide stir. He urged consideration of allowing governors more than one term and establishment of an intermediate court between the circuit level and the Supreme Court of Appeals.

Sen. Henry E. Howell, Jr. took up the cry on November 15 and Del. M. Caldwell Butler, of Roanoke, Anderson's Republican colleague, renewed agitation for a convention. On April 19, 1967, the Executive Board of the Virginia Association of Counties, joined the Anderson plea. By July 20, a survey of legislators made by Ozzie Osborn of The Roanoke World-News showed heavy support for revision. But on September 18, a year after Anderson opened the subject, Governor Godwin urged caution and in effect held that the time was not ripe.

The pressures were building, however, and by the time the 1968 General Assembly convened in January Godwin had made up his mind that the advocates for change were right. He asked at the outset for authority to appoint an 11-man Commission on Constitutional Revision.

Ditching in committee the Republican bill for a convention, the House voted 81 to 14 and the Senate 34 to 5 to grant the authority. That was January 16 and only 10 days later Godwin announced the commission membership headed by Justice Albertis S. Harrison, Jr. It included 10 lawyers, one a Republican and one a Negro, the selections being unanimously lauded by the press.

Named to the historic group were State Circuit Judge Albert V. Bryan of Fairfax, former State Sen. George M. Cochran of Staunton, former Governor Colgate W. Darden, Jr., Dean Hardy C. Dillard of the University of Virginia Law School, State Circuit Judge Alex M. Harman, Jr. of Pulaski, Oliver W. Hill of Richmond, a Negro attorney, J. Sloan Kuykendall of Winchester, Dr. Davis Y. Paschall, president of the College of William and Mary and the only non-lawyer; Lewis F. Powell, Jr., of Richmond, former president of the American Bar Association, and U. S. District Judge Ted Dalton of Radford, the only Republican and former candidate for governor.

Time now was the critical feature because the recommendations would have to be ready for a special legislative session in 1969. Passage at that time and again by the 1970 regular session would be necessary before proposed changes could go to the people in referendum.

And so Godwin wasted no time. On February 7, midway of the 1968 session, he met with the commission to launch its work and to pledge full use of state resources. As might be expected, ideas for constitutional changes began to inundate the clerk's desks in both houses. In order not to interfere with commission work, committees gave the proposals unceremonious burial. Some later were to see life renewed but not many.

On March 4 the commission made the happy choice of an executive director in the person of A. E. "Dick" Howard, associ-

Now, Here's Why We Need Money: Governor Godwin goes before the House Appropriations Committee in January 1968 to back up budget he and Budget Director L. M. Kuhn, seated center, put together.

ate dean of the University of Virginia Law School. It followed this quickly on April 7 by creating five subcommittees, each able to draw on services of specialists around the state.

These groups covered a Bill of Rights study; the executive branch and administration; legislative and judicial departments; local government, and taxation and finance.

Virginia is accustomed to special studies, particularly by sub-groups of that invaluable organization, the Virginia Advisory Legislative Council, but this probably was the most thorough-going task ever performed.

Following a series of public hearings in all parts of the State, the commission spent six months in preparing its report, a monumental 542-page document. To dramatize the importance of the work, it was presented to Governor Godwin by Justice Harrison and his colleagues in a special ceremony held in the Great Hall of the Christopher Wren Building at the College of William and Mary—a room in which the House of Burgesses had sat in colonial days after the burning of Jamestown in 1699. The report was released to press, radio and television simultaneously, consequently obtaining tremendous publicity.

The report in reality called for a rewritten Constitution, even moving some sections to the Declaration of Rights. It kept the one-term idea for governors, rejected annual legislative ses-

163

sions in favor of a 90- day biennial session, opposed lowering the voting age, set a higher minimum population for towns to become cities and asked that the State guarantee education of "high quality" in all parts of the Commonwealth.

It provided for a commission on local government as urged by the Hahn Commission, tied future bond issues and debt to revenue rather than real estate, provided two methods for issuing bonds, proposed greater supervision for public authorities and deleted many obsolete and inoperable sections.

After conferring with legislative leaders, Godwin summoned what was destined to be an historic special session of the General Assembly for February 26 and to last 59 days instead of the anticipated 30. Wisely, he restricted the call to the one subject unless there was something he wished to send down. He resisted practically every effort of well-meaning law-makers to introduce a plethora of local measures.

Praising the commission report in an address to the joint session, Godwin endorsed most of its proposals as "consistent, soundly reasoned and profoundly documented". He approved provisions for borrowing which could make available $175 to $200 million for capital needs in the 1972-75 period but questioned the idea of bond issues without a popular vote and cited his promises during the 1968 bond referendum campaign. He also differed as to the exact wording of the "high quality" education guarantee.

More succinctly, he put it this way:

"You must choose what is to be preserved from the old, and what must be accepted from the new. . . It is no longer a Virginia of magnolias and mint juleps that awaits your decision, but a Virginia at last coming into her own after nearly three-quarters of a century of wandering in the wilderness of Reconstruction and rebuilding, a Virginia now sought after by new industry and new citizens alike".

Dick Howard, the commission's executive director, did an excellent job in explaining various provisions to committees in both houses which went over the report with a fine-tooth legislative comb.

When it was over on April 25, the General Assembly had resolved to have six separate propositions on the ballot in November 1970 provided the regular 1970 legislative session agreed. Since membership would be substantially the same, this was regarded as altogether probable.

The bad examples of New York and Maryland were cited in which voters rejected new constitutions submitted in a single package, take-it-or-leave-it question.

Specific questions on the ballot were fixed by the 1969 session. Essentially they were to cover (1) whether to extend tuition grants to handicapped children in parochial schools, (2) whether to leave in the present document a section forbidding lotteries, (3) whether the General Assembly shall have power to fix the boundaries of the capital city of Richmond, (4) and (5) on issuance of general obligation and revenue bonds and (6) an all-inclusive "non-controversial" question.

(Propositions 1 and 3 were destined to be dropped by the 1970 regular session after they fell short of enough votes to get out of committees in both houses. Whether the decision allayed controversy or created new argument can be determined only when the referendum votes are counted later this year).

No. 6 would include enlargement of the Supreme Court, changes in the appointive power of circuit court judges, compulsory school attendance, guarantee of "high quality" public school education, local school cost sharing, standardization of income tax laws, restrictions on towns becoming cities, consumer protection and tax deferrals.

Among the chief changes from the commission report was the decision to hold 60-day sessions in even-numbered years and 30- day sessions in odd-numbered years, each extendable by 30 days on three-fourths vote of both houses.

The Hahn Commission's idea for a Commission on Local Government is left in status that the Assembly "may" create one if it desires. Like the Supreme Court, the State Board of Education would be increased from 7 to 9 members.

One of the most notable of several teapot tempests was stirred by Sen. Henry E. Howell's proposal to eliminate the word "Christian" in the Declaration of Rights phrase where the Founding Fathers urged one another to practice "Christian forebearance". Churchmen became involved on both sides as well as the non-religious. The phrase stayed.

Pleased with the outcome, Governor Godwin saw in the final work the erection of another capstone to his administration, provided the 1970 session and the people approve.

"I know of nothing that is going to be more important to the long future of Virginia than the recommendations of the commission and the Assembly's approval of them", he summarized.

Who should bear the burden of trying to "sell" the electorate and obtaining referendum approval of the new Constitution?

Godwin is willing to help if called upon. Indeed, he probably could not avoid the temptation to participate in the campaign but he believes Governor Holton rightfully should lead the way and that he will have tremendous bipartisan support.

One thing is perfectly evident: the 1902 Constitution, even with the amendments of 1928 and subsequent thereto, is outmoded. It is somewhat like the horse and buggy in a nuclear and space age.

THE FLYING GOVERNOR

In former years the people of Virginia seldom saw their governor after the campaigning was over and he was inaugurated, especially in the far reaches of the State beyond easy driving distance from Richmond. Even with good roads, some of them were just too far away for him to pay visits except for the most unusual events.

All that was changed in 1968 after Governor Godwin requested the General Assembly to provide funds for purchase of an airplane to be assigned for use of the Governor as well as the Division of Industrial Development and other state departments on a priority basis.

Not only was it necessary that the Governor get out more into all areas of the State to keep in touch with its needs but the fierce competition for industry between states demanded that he have the means of demonstrating availability of sites.

The answer lay in purchase of a Beechcraft King Air B-90 turbo-prop plane, pressurized, with all electronic equipment of big commercial jets and with cruising speed of up to 250 mph. It cost $484,000 on discount from the list price of $535,000.

It is flown by pilots attached to the Division of Aeronautics under the State Corporation Commission, headed by Col. Willard F. Plentl and his assistant, Maj. Kenneth Rowe, with four other pilots who also fly the State's two-motor Aztec capable of carrying four passengers with crew of two.

Plane that made Godwin Governor of all Virginia: Col. Willard F. Plentl, right, and Maj. Kenneth Rowe, left, pose in front of the Beechcraft King Air which paid for itself in the first year of service.

The King Air can carry eight besides pilot and copilot when there is no baggage or 5 to 6 passengers with reasonable baggage.

"It is one of the best investments the State has ever made", observes Godwin. "It has more than paid for itself several times over because of what we have been able to do in showing Virginia to some of the top management people from outside the State whose time was limited and yet who wanted to see various places in Virginia.

"It has served a highly useful purpose and I hardly know how we got along without it for so long. It has enabled me to go many places in Virginia. We now have 92 licensed airports in the State and the plane has enabled me to go into areas I could not possibly have gotten into otherwise because of lack of time.

"There was some criticism of the purchase, as we had expected, but it has been relatively insignificant. During the 1968 bond campaign we heard a few critical remarks but these apparently had very little adverse effect".

Major Rowe estimates that when Godwin's term ended he had flown between 175 and 180 hours, all within the borders of the State, for a total of 45,150 miles. The Division of Industrial Development and the Division of State Planning and Community Affairs had used the plane about an equal amount.

Something of what benefits flowed in dollars and cents as a result of having the plane is offered by William C. Sims, assistant director of the Division of Industrial Development:

"The availability of a private plane has become increasingly important in promoting the location of industry throughout the State. The industrial executive has limited time available and yet must look at numerous locations before making a decision. Happily, he is very much interested in the many locations throughout the State located away from our major metropolitan areas and which do not have scheduled air service. Through the use of State planes, the executive need have no hesitancy in scheduling visits to the many areas, no matter how remote, in which he may be interested. We feel the use of the plane has been of definite assistance in encouraging industry to consider our more rural areas as well as the metropolitan centers.

"The first official use of the new King Air was by the Division of Industrial Development to fly officials of Imperial Chemical Industries to various sites in Virginia. ICI recently announced their decision to locate a $50 million plant at Bermuda Hundred (on the James River). The next day the plane was used in connection with our efforts to locate Anheuser-Busch in Virginia.

Again, a $40 million complex in the Williamsburg area was the result.

"During the slightly over one year that the plane has been available to us, it has been used to assist in the location of seven plants in Virginia representing a planned investment in excess of $150 million.

"In addition, we have had officials of nine different companies in the plane during this period who are still actively considering locating within the State. The potential involved could be in excess of $100 million. It is interesting to note that relatively few of the industrial prospects involved have failed to locate within the State".

The Governor, of course, endeavored to separate politics from State business where use of the plane was concerned. The $81 million bond referendum campaign for college and mental hospital construction was considered nonpartisan because the bond money was to benefit directly or indirectly all citizens of the Commonwealth.

As noted elsewhere, Mr. Godwin pressed the campaign with vigor while recovering from the tragic loss of his daughter, and spoke frequently in every part of the State, sometimes as many as three and four times a day.

Governor and Becky return from Expo '67 at Montreal. She didn't like to fly but changed her mind to go with Daddy and they had a great time.

—Richmond Newspapers Photo

This would not have been possible without the King Air, capable of landing and taking off on the dozens of small airfields, one being within reasonable driving distance of almost every town and village.

In addition, Godwin was enabled to accept scores of invitations which otherwise might have had to be rejected. The plane could get him across the State and back to its home port, Byrd Field at Richmond, in a matter of minutes.

Thus it was that he probably dedicated more schools and industrial plants than any two or three previous governors combined.

In this manner he became the Flying Governor, seen and heard in person by more Virginians than any predecessor. This in turn inevitably added to his popularity and, more than anything else, gave the people a greater sense of closeness to their state government. It was no longer something far removed and never seen in action.

A pattern has been set which future governors are likely to find impossible to change, at least very much.

1969 PRIMARIES AND THE GREAT SCHISM

It was an odd quirk of fate that 1969, Mills E. Godwin's final year in the governorship, was also destined to mark widening of a growing schism in the Democratic Party, a collapse of what remained of the once all-powerful Byrd Machine and the first election of a Republican governor in 84 years.

Historians will be trying for years to decide exactly what happened and why, whether it happened because of Democratic weakness or Republican strength, or whether it would have happened had Mills Godwin been willing and able to transfer his magic to other shoulders.

It all began early in 1968. Lt. Gov. Fred G. Pollard was not unaware that Godwin had set his sights on the top job before the Harrison administration was half over and that Harrison obviously favored Godwin for his successor. While Godwin had not chosen Pollard to run on the same ticket in 1965 neither had he offered discouragement.

Thus it was that the 1968 legislative session saw Pollard busy trying to line up support among the law-makers, a time-honored maneuver. He was aware that Sen. Henry E. Howell, Jr. of Norfolk was threatening to run, that William C. Battle, son of former Gov. John S. Battle of Charlottesville, was making noises like a candidate and that there was even mention of Dr. T. Marshall Hahn, the personable and widely-popular president of VPI.

Pollard almost had his mind made up to announce right after the Democratic State convention at Salem in July, 1968, but Godwin advised him that this was far too early and he waited until August, still about the earliest on record.

A month later, Battle announced as the hopeful of moderates in the party, fully expecting Howell to carry the liberal banner, which proved to be the case. All three apparently wanted to keep Dr. Hahn from taking the plunge. The question in many minds has been: what deterred him?

There is not much doubt that the Virginia Tech president had considerable support in business and industrial circles but he never mustered enough among the politicians where it counts.

His own position was that the time was not right but he probably would have entered the race had Pollard been willing to withdraw, believing that he could beat Battle and Howell in a showdown. He felt he could be a unifying force in the face of a threatening split.

The one thing Dr. Hahn wanted most, of course, was public endorsement by Governor Godwin but this was never forthcoming. They were close friends, Hahn having backed the Godwin programs and in particular stumping the state for the $81 million college-hospital bond issue.

With Dr. Hahn's agreement, Godwin disclosed what happened. They talked numerous times, Hahn making clear his interest in running if he could get the proper support, which, of course, meant Organization backing and Godwin endorsement. Cautiously, Godwin advised a thorough examination of the situation, especially with General Assembly members.

Leaders in the Assembly gave little satisfaction. In fact, three members favorably disposed—Senators Lloyd C. Bird, George McMath and Paul Manns—are believed to have made a study for him and rendered an unfavorable report.

Leaders in higher education proved to be unenthusiastic, indeed even jealous. The chief drum-beater for Hahn's cause, Roanoke businessman John W. Hancock, did some high-pressure work but proved a bit naive about practical politics. He appears to have irritated some with the intimation that he would support A. Linwood Holton, the Republican, if Hahn did not run.

Hahn's insistence on Godwin's public endorsement if he was to make the race proved to be the big stumbling block.

"This bothered me because it involved a governor picking his successor and it involved Fred Pollard who had been extremely loyal to me while I was governor in getting support for my programs in the General Assembly. I was not hostile to Bill Battle although we had been at odds on some issues".

His feelings about Howell were well-known, of course, and in view of the election of William B. Spong, Jr. to the U. S. Senate in 1966, he would have expected much of the Spong strength to go to Battle rather than Howell, or if Howell did not run, all would go to Battle.

Never choosing between Battle and Pollard, the Governor tried repeatedly to get what he termed "an accommodation" between them—one or the other to withdraw or to run for lieutenant governor. He did indicate in one talk that he felt experience in the General Assembly constituted superior qualification and this could have applied only to Pollard.

"However, I knew that Pollard was not stirring up enthusiasm that he thought his candidacy would create. I did not necessarily feel that he would be a winner or even among the top two. I further felt that the only way that he could win in a three-way race was for Battle to be eliminated in the first primary —that a runoff between Battle and Pollard would in all probability have been a victory for Battle. The people supporting

Howell in the first inevitably would turn to Battle in the runoff if his opponent had been Pollard".

Thus it was that speculation tended more and more to center on Hahn as a compromise candidate. Again Godwin told his friend that he doubted the wisdom of an endorsement which might hurt rather than help.

According to Godwin, Hahn then asked if he could let leaders in the General Assembly and political circles know of his preference without saying so publicly. Godwin replied that this would be tantamount to a public announcement and this he shied away from. By this time (February) Godwin felt it was too late anyhow and that Hahn's financial problem would be almost insurmountable.

Shortly thereafter Dr. Hahn issued a statement in which he decided to stick to higher education. He still thinks he could have

Hahn's Off

won. In retrospect, Godwin now also thinks that perhaps Hahn might have been victorious.

The primaries were almost, but not quite, anti-climactic after this long suspense drama.

Looking back on that protracted period of indecision, Godwin commented: "Dr. Hahn would have been a formidable candidate. He was most fluent and intellectually a giant. But the lines had been drawn and he would have had to leave VPI at great personal cost—there was just too much risk involved".

And so, it was a three-man race after all in the first round of July 15—Pollard the conservative, Battle the moderate and Howell the liberal—each sure he could win for different reasons. Pollard expected to get the Byrd and Willis Robertson vote while Battle and Howell would split the vote that William B. Spong, Jr. had mustered in whipping Senator Robertson.

Battle felt he would draw from both right and left, deriving considerable strength from the connections of his father, and getting help from Spong, who he had supported in 1966.

Howell, of course, was the champion of organized labor and was drawing heavily from the Negro vote with his assaults on the sales tax, especially as it applied to food and non-prescription drugs. He made a great to-do with a borrowed slogan: "Keep the Big Boys Honest!" The Big Boys were never fully identified.

One of the oddities of the first primary campaign was the diligence with which candidates tried to get under the "Godwin umbrella".

Pollard coined the phrase in a speech when he laid claim to standing under it as a firm supporter of the Governor's progressive legislative program and as one who had helped engineer it.

Battle rather promptly embraced the Godwin program and said he, too, was under the umbrella because he intended to further the program.

Howell held a press conference thereafter, declaring that Godwin had no right to hold an umbrella over any candidate and besides, if there was an umbrella, it had been invented by the progressives, more specifically Henry Howell.

The contention became so keen that Ed Grimsley, writing in the Richmond Times-Dispatch of July 4, predicted that an umbrella would win the primaries and probably be elected Governor Nov. 4.

Godwin followed the tradition of Virginia governors in remaining silent, having made his position on Howell clear but refusing to choose publicly between Battle and Pollard. Referring to Howell, he observed early in 1969:

"I do not think his nomination or election would be in the best interests of Virginia and I do not agree with his general philosophy of government and I cannot give him my support in the primary. I stopped short of ever saying that I would not vote for Mr. Howell if he were the nominee of the Democratic Party".

Some of Howell's lieutenants tried hard to compel Godwin to pledge that he would support the nominee regardless but this the Governor resisted by saying that he always had supported the nominee of his party in past elections.

If Pollard's political philosophy was closer to his own than that of the other two men, why did he not support the lieutenant governor?

The answer is that Godwin doubted Pollard could win even with Godwin's all-out support.

"All my information by early July was that Mr. Pollard was going to run third but I personally felt that Mr. Battle was going to be stronger in the first primary than he turned out to be.

"This was despite my personal feeling that Fred was an extremely capable individual. His knowledge of state government was not equalled by either of the other candidates and he had the character and qualifications needed to be a good governor. But he did not possess those warm personal attributes to make him an attractive campaigner. This, more than any other one thing, I think, worked toward his defeat".

The outcome was a shocker to many including the Governor, Bill Battle and more especially Pollard, who ran third by 60,000 while less than 5,000 separated Howell from Battle, the front runner. The vote: Battle 159,000; Howell 154,000; Pollard 95,000.

There was now a five-week intermission for a runoff primary —the first to be held since enactment of a law following the 1949 victory of John S. Battle in a four-way primary with Horace H.

175

Edwards, Col. Francis Pickens Miller and Remmie L. Arnold. Sen. J. Sargeant Reynolds with 236,000 had won easy nomination for lieutenant governor over W. C. Thompson with 87,000, Herman (Hard Times) Hunt with 27,000 and Moses A. Riddick with 20,000, but Andrew P. Miller was forced into a runoff for attorney general by Guy O. Farley, who really never had much chance to win. The vote: Miller 152,000; Farley 130,00; Bernard Levin 47,000; C. F. Hicks 41,000.

Bill Battle was in Godwin's office the morning after the first primary asking for support in the runoff, support which the Governor promptly announced to a press conference the day after. Godwin was sure Howell could not win in November.

Three weeks after the July 15 vote the Governor addressed a $35 per plate luncheon at the John Marshall Hotel for which 800 tickets were sold and 650 appeared. Joseph E. Blackburn, as chairman, together with E. Angus Powell of Richmond, and Matt Anderson of Goochland, did a solid job of rallying the conservative and moderate forces.

It was a big boost financially for Battle who was heavily in debt and needed at least $85,000 more for the runoff. Godwin addressed a breakfast for 250 at Arlington the morning before the runoff as a further gesture.

The second primary August 19 found the electorate dog-tired from more than a year of campaigning and nursing a bad case of tin ear. The final result was a Battle margin of 21,000 (225,000 to 204,000) but it was to prove a Pyrrhic victory. Miller whipped Farley by 103,000 or 247,000 to 144,000.

REPUBLICANS BREAK AN 84-YEAR DROUGHT

It was a tired and financially-strapped William C. Battle with a Democratic Party badly split three ways who now went into the general election campaign against a fresh, confident and well-heeled Republican candidate named Abner Linwood Holton, Jr.

Holton, a native of Big Stone Gap, like Battle a Navy veteran and popular young attorney, had earned his political spurs under the redoubtable Ted Dalton by running for local offices and then making an excellent showing by coming in second in the 1965 gubernatorial race won by Mills Godwin.

As usual, the Republicans had nominated their slate at a convention, this time even before the opposition primaries got under way, picking Sen. H. D. "Buz" Dawbarn of Waynesboro to run for lieutenant governor and Richard D. Obenshain of Richmond for attorney general.

The convention method had a lot to commend it, chiefly this time that it was a lot cheaper than primaries and it prevented any weaknesses from being exhibited publicly for such a long time.

The GOP had run a full slate for the top state offices for years but, except for the Dalton and Holton efforts, without much hope or expectation. Since World War II they had been concentrating on General Assembly seats and local offices, building from the grass roots, as the politicians put it.

They had done a remarkable job, as events were to prove, in cultivating youth and seeking the woman's vote.

Having carried the state in every presidential election since 1948 (except in 1964) climaxed with the election of Richard M. Nixon in 1968, they now found campaign financing much easier.

Holton and his slate waged a vigorous campaign centering on the theme: "It's Time for a Change", but carefully refrained from attacking the Godwin record, largely perhaps because Holton had approved of just about all of it except extending the sales tax to food and patent medicines.

Says Godwin, looking back:

177

"I was pleased that none of the candidates in any of the elections in 1969 took any sharp issue with the policies and programs of my administration. In fact, even Holton, when he announced for Governor early in the year, said that if I could run for reelection, he might not run because of my good record".

It is interesting to note that the polls made by the several candidates indicated popular acceptance in high degree (63-65 pct) of the Godwin programs. Godwin had occasion to see polls taken for Battle in both primary and general election campaigns, as well as that taken by Pollard in the first primary.

The general tenor of the GOP plea was that the Republicans could do a better job of continuing the progress started by Godwin.

For his part, Godwin was mystified by the plea. Time for a change from what? He had furnished plenty of change, in fact, the greatest change in over 40 years.

What happened, then?

"I think when it's all summed up and the record is written years from now", says Godwin, "it will be obvious that Mr. Battle failed and his campaign failed because they were unable to convince the people that a *great deal of change* had occurred in the past four years".

"The truth is that *we had had about as much change* in Virginia from 1966 to 1970 *as the state could possibly absorb.* I don't think this point was ever gotten across by Battle and his organization".

There were a lot more reasons than that, of course.

Battle was saddled with the onus of having defeated the Organization candidate (Pollard) in the first primary. He was unable to win back many of the old line conservatives. Large numbers actually and publicly went over to Holton.

It was obvious that Senator Howell took his defeat in the runoff with great bitterness. While he would vote for Battle because of the primary candidate pledge, he made his supporters "free agents" and never made any addresses for Battle. Once he conferred with the party candidate and reportedly demanded a pledge of 40 per cent of appointments for his wing of the party should Battle win. Battle refused.

But Howell's sharpest barbs were reserved for Governor

Godwin and Rep. Watkins M. Abbitt, the state chairman, who were, in his opinion, driving out liberals and destroying the party.

Godwin's reaction: "I was rather complimented that he felt I had that much influence".

The AFL-CIO and the Crusade of Voters, the latter a Richmond Negro organization, both of which had supported Howell in both primaries, came out for Holton with the announced purpose of getting rid of the last vestiges of the Byrd Organization.

At the same time these bodies backed Democrats J. Sargeant Reynolds for lieutenant governor and Andrew P. Miller for attorney general. The fact that all three of their men won is strong indication of the power they exerted.

Here we turn to Godwin's assessment made for the writer two weeks after the election:

"Mr. Battle obviously was caught in a political squeeze in that he lost the vote of liberals who thought he was tied too close to the old Byrd Organization and to the status quo, while some conservatives deserted to the Republican ranks because they felt he was tied too closely to the National Democratic Party.

"The Conservatives also disliked his connection with the Kennedys and national Democratic leaders, his statement that he would support the National Democratic nominee in 1972 and his statement that he would try to help restructure the National Democratic Party when his voice would only be a voice in the wilderness attempting to do that.

"It was obvious that the National Democratic Party could not help him any in the election. It would have been a disaster of vast proportion to have invited any of those leaders into the state to campaign for him.

"Exactly the reverse was true so far as Mr. Holton was concerned because the National Republican Party now in power is fairly popular in Virginia. Mr. Nixon had always carried the state when he ran. He was able to do quite well in 1968. His policies are in accord with the thinking of many Virginians and this was a great plus factor for Holton.

"Mr. Nixon's visit to Roanoke and Salem the week before the election was also a plus factor with its large crowd and tremendous publicity which sparked a lot of momentum for Holton.

179

RICHMOND TIMES-DISPATCH

"I think also that the President's speech on Vietnam the night before the election had a tremendous impact on Virginia voters. It reached great numbers of "swing voters" who vote on the basis of personalities and issues rather than party affiliations.

"He didn't say much about how to settle the conflict but he said much to promote unity in the country. This, coming on the heels of the Vietnam moratorium demonstrations, did a lot to solidify thinking toward Holton because of his close alliance with Mr. Nixon.

"Mr. Battle lacked broad-based financial support and this partly contributed to his defeat—he could not field an organization comparable to those of the past. He had problems financing

180

his own primary campaign and his resources were exhausted by the time of the general campaign. Had it not been for the aid of the old line conservatives he hardly would have had money to have concluded his campaign.

"Also, there was an impression abroad that there was 'not a great deal of difference between Holton and Battle'—people looked on them as having the same philosophy of government. They equated them as individuals in capacity and both as inexperienced in government.

"A lot of people, feeling this to be true and the Republican Party not having had a governorship in 85 years decided it wouldn't hurt to let them try it for four years to see what they could do with it".

Governor Godwin was not overly surprised, therefore, when Holton swept to victory, the final vote being: Holton, 481,000; Battle, 415,000. Reynolds snowed Dawbarn 472,000 to 388,000 and Miller soundly whipped Obenshain 455,000 to 402,000.

In retrospect—in fact, in the midst of the campaign—it was apparent to Godwin that the Democratic Party—and it's hard to distinguish the party from the now defunct Byrd Organization— had developed a well-nigh fatal flaw. It had failed to develop new and vigorous leadership within its ranks ready to assume the burdens of government.

There are those who contend that the Organization discouraged new talent, particularly if the individual found himself unable "to stay in line". Godwin himself had some little experience along this line but managed to survive it and climb to the top.

But the fact remains that the Organization did produce good men—perhaps not always progressive enough, but men who gave honest government and who lived within the means which the people were willing to provide.

Fragmentation of the party in the wake of Byrd's passing and the close of Godwin's remarkably achieving administration pose a problem of survival.

With this problem we shall deal in a subsequent chapter.

WHAT NOW FOR DEMOCRATS?

Mills Godwin had cause for surprisingly few regrets when he stepped out of office in January after what was probably the most productive governorship of the Twentieth Century but there was one that caused him much chagrin . . . he was the first among 22 governors unable to leave a Democratic successor.

There was no question but what the defeat of William C. Battle by Republican Linwood Holton had left the Democratic party with shattered ranks and shaken to the foundations of its stronghold despite election of J. Sargeant Reynolds as lieutenant governor and Andrew Pickens Miller as attorney general.

To understand fully what has happened, observed Godwin in surveying the shambles, it is necessary to look first of all at relationships between the National and State Democratic Parties . . . they have been out of tune for over 30 years with only one presidential candidate (Johnson) able to carry the state since Roosevelt. And it was Godwin who helped perform that miracle.

"The overwhelming number of people in Virginia are conservative or moderately conservative", says Godwin. "They are realistic. They are progressive in the sense that they want to be progressive on a conservative basis. They want to pay their debts. They want to borrow no more money than they need to borrow. They don't want to spend any more in their budget than is necessary for the critical and essential needs of the state.

"This has made the majority of people in both parties in Virginia at variance with the underlying philosophy of much of the majority of the National Democratic Party. This is reflected in many ways and by the delegations in both House and Senate".

There has been some moderation in this view, he admits, and it first became evident in the state convention at Salem in 1968 when liberals and moderates gained control of the State Central Committee.

Godwin expects the leadership to continue as constituted with Rep. Watkins M. Abbitt, a conservative, as chairman, and State Sen. William B. Hopkins, a moderate, as national committeeman. Although moderates and liberals together might hold control at times, he expects the moderates to weld with the conservatives rather than in the other direction.

"Consistently more of the conservative candidates are elected", reflects the Governor. "I think it very interesting to note that in five districts now having Republican congressmen a liberal Democrat was defeated".

Specifically, he cited the win of William L. Whitehurst in 1968, a conservative Democrat only four years before, over Fred T. Stant, a Howell ally in the Second District fight; William Scott's triumph over George C. Rawlings, who had ended the long 8th District tenure of Rep. Howard W. Smith in the primary; Joel T. Broyhill's easy wins over Gus Johnson and Clive Duvall in the 10th, and William C. Wampler's tremendous majority over Pat Jennings in the "Fighting Ninth".

"And in the Sixth, Democrats couldn't find an opponent last time for conservative Republican Richard H. Poff", Godwin adds.

"None of the three nominees in Virginia in 1969 would have dared ask for help from leaders of the National Democratic Party.

"Virginia overwhelmingly is moderately conservative. So long as the National Democratic Party continues its liberal, free-spending, inflationary policies, I see no reason to think that the people of Virginia, even in the Democratic Party, are going to give them much help. Liberal candidates are going to continue to be defeated statewide. You will see some stay in the General Assembly because in some urban and more populous rural areas their elections are going to occur, but you will continue to see domination by conservative and moderate forces.

"In many ways what happened in 1969 will rejuvenate the party, add strength to it, and make us more mindful of the fact that we cannot take elections for granted . . . that the Democratic nomination is no longer tantamount to election and that we are going to have to fight in every election . . . in many ways the party will be strengthened rather than weakened . . . I think you are going to see a party that is vibrant and vigorous for a long time to come . . . it's had too fine a record of service to be otherwise".

Godwin added that he fully agreed with Rep. J. Vaughan Gary's remarks on WRVA Radio the night of the election after

Holton's victory became apparent, that while disappointed, he predicted that four years from now Virginians would realize what good government they had under the Democrats.

But there was something which worried the Governor as it must worry every politician and student of government: the rising cost of getting elected to high office in Virginia.

Total official spending for both parties when November 4 arrived was estimated at $2.7 million, but if all outlays were included the figure probably was closer to $3.5 million, maybe more. Spending by all candidates and their followers in the two Democratic primaries likely hit $2 million. The official Republican cost of electing Holton was $500,000 but all GOP spending doubtless exceeded $1 million.

Like just about everyone else, Godwin frowns and says "something must be done" to lower the price on office in the State, but what?

If a runoff is kept, he says, the period between first primary and runoff must be shortened. "People get tired of the campaigning and crowds at rallies become poor".

It may be necesary to place legal limits on spending, he adds.

Pointing out that television has become a major source of expense, the donation of equal time to candidates by stations is about the only cost-cutter he can see.

Of one thing he is positive: "campaigns should not be financed out of the public purse".

What happened November 4 other than the fact that Holton won?

Mr. Godwin already had mentioned the shift of the labor and black votes which put a split ticket into office. But there was something else. It was obvious, be admitted ruefully, that "we did not take youth into account".

Does that mean that the Democrats have lost them? Not really.

Like Patrick Henry, who was first Governor under the Commonwealth, Godwin believes that the only lamp by which feet of his party can be guided in the future is past experience.

"We have to get more young people involved in the party processes, let them be part of the apparatus, get some of them

184

to run for office as Democrats, let them know they are welcome and their leadership desired.

"If there is one political fault that can be laid to the long-time dominant Organization it was the unwillingness to permit younger people to have a greater part in the major policy-making processes of the party and to be actively identified with it.

"I don't make this as a blanket indictment because I'm an exception and came up through the Organization as did many others, young in years and good Democrats, whose leadership is very much in evidence.

"At the same time we've permitted others who wanted to be identified in politics to get away from us because they couldn't find a home like they wanted in the Democratic Party. They felt the party was not responsive and responsible enough".

Beyond this Godwin preferred to await developments and withheld further comment except on the subject of prospects for reelection of Sen. Harry F. Byrd, Jr., with which we shall deal in the following chapter.

*   *   *

Shad Planking at Waverly is rivaled only by the famed Byrd Apple Orchard Picnic for getting politicians and would-be politicians together. Here, Godwin addresses some 3000 at one of Sen. Garland Gray's shindings.

—Richmond Newspapers Photo

It seems necessary to this record and analysis that we look beyond the Governor's recapitulation for a glimpse of what may lie in store for his party.

As a long-time observer of the scene, the author offers some comment on his own, much of it gleaned from others just as familiar with what the late Frank Kent called "The Great Game of Politics".

First of all, it has been proven time and again on national, state and local levels that a single, seemingly devastating defeat need not necessarily mean the demise of a powerful, long-entrenched political machine. Sometimes a good solid shellacking at the polls can do more to revitalize an organization and help its leaders see their faults than anything else.

While it is true that the Republicans, riding the flying coattails of Linwood Holton, captured 24 seats in the House of Delegates and subsequently picked up another Senate seat for a total of seven, Democrats still hold an overwhelming majority of 75 in the House and 33 in the Senate. (There is one independent delegate).

It is inconceivable that a party with 108 of the 140 seats in the General Assembly should be thought, even by the most naive, incapable of bringing forward new leadership.

Nobody expects the badly defeated Battle to step into the breach because he has no base of operations at the seat of government. Rather, it must be expected that leadership will develop from the legislative ranks. It cannot come from men in the executive department under Republican control.

There are three leading prospects, of course, by virtue of their position: Speaker John Warren Cooke of Mathews in the House, Lt. Gov. Reynolds and Atty. Gen. Miller.

Of these three, Cooke is the only man with any solid experience and he holds by far the most powerful and influential post. Reynolds and Miller still have to prove themselves in action.

But it is unnecessary to sit in any of those jobs to move up the ladder. Harry Byrd, Sr. was the best example of how a young, ambitious and capable man can skip all that.

Some of the leadership, especially in the Senate, is on the aging side but there are younger "comers" like Hunter Andrews of Hampton and Bill Hopkins of Roanoke.

186

In the House are many good men who, by holding powerful committee chairmanships or key positions, are capable of moving out in front any time. There are Roy Smith of Petersburg, James M. Thomson of Alexandria, Lewis McMurran of Newport News, Wick Anderson of Roanoke, French Slaughter of Culpeper and Ed Lane of Richmond, to name just a few.

With a strong man like Godwin in the Governor's chair, it was almost inevitable that many a potential strong light was obscured by the bushel.

It was not surprising that there would be drifting at start of a new legislative session when the Democratic Party had been rendered rudderless. It was natural, too, that there should be factional squabbling such as that which manifested itself in the Senate in the effort of conservatives, led by Sen. Edward L. Breeden, of Norfolk, to keep Lt. Gov. Reynolds off the Rules Committee.

All three factions—Conservatives, Moderates and Liberals —soon began realizing that they had to cooperate within the General Assembly. There is growing awareness that the pending fight over Harry Byrd's Senate seat in July could be a fatal luxury.

As Governor Godwin says, the Liberal wing is weaker, if anything, since November. Henry Howell remains its leader on the Hill but he is rather lonesome. The Conservatives and Moderates are stronger and beginning to understand that they must work together.

From all indications, the trend is toward moderation. This faction undoubtedly demonstrated superiority in the 1970 General Assembly.

Something will emerge to replace the Byrd Organization. That is a political fact of life. If those who sought so diligently to destroy the long-dominant Machine were to gain the upper hand, they would substitute an organization of their own. That stems from the basic desire to control and to remain in power.

For the present, however, the Democratic Party has to be acknowledged in sad disarray.

For the first time in a long while it is sinking home with Democrats of all hues that they must get back to "grass root" organization and vote-cultivation. For more than eight decades the "courthouse rings" had taken care of that. Now they have been outmaneuvered by the Republicans whose precinct-level work paid off in November 1969.

That vote forced realization, too, that the large Negro and organized labor bloc votes no longer could be taken for granted. They shifted to the GOP and spelled the difference.

Governor Holton now is cultivating both assiduously, especially the black vote, and it will not be regained easily.

It is evident also to the more discerning Democrats that they lost altogether too much of the youth support, not just last year, but in growing numbers over recent years. As Mr. Godwin says, it is going to be necessary to cultivate these again and lure them back while concentrating on the thousands who each year come of voting age.

Still holding a vast majority of local offices across the State, the Party has a firm nucleus but is going to need much more imagination than it has displayed of late.

Somehow, too, it must halt the defection of older Conservatives who still constitute a majority in most instances.

None of this is going to be easy.

As this is written, Democrats in all parts of the State are looking to the General Assembly for emergence of new leadership, fully aware that a Mills Godwin is an infrequent occurrence.

DON'T COUNT 'THE CHAMP' OUT

Just because he retired undefeated from the political ring on January 17, 1970, is no reason to assume that Mills E. Godwin, Jr. cannot be persuaded to run again for public office.

True, like all his predecessors, he turns the phrase: "Governor of Virginia" over lovingly in his mind and on his tongue.

The Champ in a Happy Moment.

"There is no higher honor within the gift of the people of this Commonwealth", he says almost reverently. So say they all.

But what about the immediate problem of leadership in the Democratic Party?

"I have no desire as the most recent Governor to be the political leader in Virginia", he responds with candor. "I have no base from which to operate but I'm not going to be devoid of interest in the fortunes of the party".

At 55, Godwin is in his vigorous prime physically and mentally and after 22 years in politics it is inconceivable that he has lost all of his desire for public service.

His old law firm, founded by his late cousin, Charles B. Godwin, and from which he resigned upon assuming the goverorship, is still there in Suffolk, headed by partner, J. Samuel Glasscock, now a member of the House of Delegates. Other members are Jeff L. Gardy and William R. Savage, III.

For a time Godwin will make that firm's offices his headquarters but he doesn't feel that he can practice before the Suffolk bar because one judge of the Circuit, James C. Godwin. is a cousin appointed by Governor Harrison and the other, Judge George F. Whitley, was appointed by Governor Godwin himself. Practicing under such circumstances, he feels, would be difficult.

Godwin is likewise aware that to practice before the Virginia Supreme Court of Appeals where he appointed three of the seven members—more than any other governor of modern times —presents a situation he would like to avoid.

On his last day in office, he spoke jokingly with the press about being unemployed but that, we may rest assured, was to be only a temporary condition.

A man of his prominence, attainments and ability would be in great demand among major corporations who could offer substantial salary and position from which to remain in the public eye. A month after leaving office he had been named to the boards of directors of two major corporations—Standard Brands, Inc. and the Norfolk and Western Railway. Standard Brands is parent of Planters Peanut Co., which is headquartered in Suffolk.

Two other even more remunerative connections followed. In early March it was announced that he would join the board of the Virginia National Bank, a Norfolk institution, with special duties in connection with industrial development and expansion of usages for port facilities.

Immediately thereafter came word that he also was joining Reynolds Metals, Inc., the great Richmond-based firm, in a capacity which will make use of his legal talents in advisory work.

He will, therefore, be just as busy as he wants to be while leaving some time for civic endeavor and for keeping an eye on the political scene, especially fortunes of the Democratic Party.

Home, at least for the foreseeable future, will continue to be in Nansemond County for the Godwins are building a new house at Cedar Point Club which they helped organize. It is situated on the Nansemond River about equi-distant from Portsmouth and Suffolk and only five miles from Chuckatuck.

The big brick home in Chuckatuck is being sold. Katherine Godwin spent one night there after Becky's passing and has not been able since to bear the thought of living there again. There were too many memories of the child that seared the heart. Anyhow, the new home is within easy driving distance of Richmond, Norfolk and other population centers. The club has become a popular place of residence for professional people from Norfolk, Portsmouth and Suffolk.

Katherine Godwin thinks her husband will find it hard to shun or escape politics for long and she is confident that he is still interested in government.

In some respects they were not sorry to leave the Mansion. The suffering and tragedy they had endured took away all of its glamour. Yet, after four years in the spotlight with all its attendant publicity, Godwin had to admit a sense of depression in cutting off the associations in government which he had found so personally rewarding.

But, if his interest in politics is to continue, where will it be based?

Repeatedly, in the last few weeks of his governorship, reporters tried to draw him out but with little success except on one subject: the Fourth District congressional seat now held by his close friend, Watkins M. Abbitt, chairman of the Democratic State Central Committee. (There had been rumors that Abbitt might retire in his favor).

Said Godwin to the author during an interview in mid-January:

"I would not be a candidate for this particular office under any circumstances I can foresee. I would not be interested for a number of reasons".

These reasons he listed as (1) His age—at 55 he would not want to be starting in the House; (2) the district is so large that campaigning in it and representing it would be a physical strain; and (3) It would take years to attain any real prominence in the House.

If Abbitt had been entertaining any thoughts of relinquishing his seat at 61 and affording Godwin an "inside track" to the Democratic nomination, this stand by the retiring Governor evidently helped make up his mind. He announced on February 22 that he would seek another two-year term.

That leaves only the U. S. Senate as a possibility in the immediate future. Harry F. Byrd, Jr. is up for reelection in 1970 and William B. Spong in 1972. Reminded of the persistent rumors originating among Democratic liberals that Byrd might turn Republican, in which event Godwin would oppose him, the Governor spoke with conviction:

He expected Byrd to remain a Democrat, planned to support him for reelection and believed that he will win a full six-year term.

"In my opinion, the outcome November 4 (1969) worked to the advantage of Senator Byrd and his renomination in the 1970 primary as well as his election next fall. His primary opposition will be from the liberal fringe—those who identify with Senator Howell.

(By mid-February two candidates already were in the field for the primary—George C. Rawlings of Fredericksburg and Alvin Edelson of Charlottesville—while two earlier aspirants had pulled out.)

"I do not believe that a candidate from this wing can defeat Byrd. He will get not only the conservative vote but, if need be, there will be enough Republicans and independents coming into the primary to rescue him.

"More importantly, those who identify themselves as moderates will go for Byrd. They realize that Senator Howell cannot reshape the party and offer nominees who can win.

"Senator Byrd and I share a political philosophy which is akin . . . I may not have agreed with every position he has taken on every issue, nor do I think that he has agreed with me about every one . . . this is understandable where you have to face numbers of public issues . . . but Senator Byrd and I have been political allies and personal friends almost all our adult lives. We came to the General Assembly together in 1948, he to the Senate and I to the House, and for ten years we were deskmates in the Senate. We enjoyed a close relationship. He supported me in every campaign and gave me much help."

All the foregoing, of course, involved speculation and reflection by the Governor only a matter of a few hours before leaving office. He could not have anticipated that on March 17 Byrd would announce refusal to sign the Democratic loyalty oath which had been adopted by the State Central Committee in February and required of candidates, but would run as an independent Democrat rather than enter the primary.

Godwin learned of the decision from his friend in person during the preceding weekend. Along with other party leaders he was shocked and dismayed.

"I regret Senator Byrd has found it necessary to take the position he has in connection with the Senatorial election in Virginia this year", he told the press. "I would not, at this time, attempt to pass judgment on his decision".

But he found it necessary to emphasize that he was not interested in opposing Byrd. This was despite the fact that Democrats of all hues seemed willing to concede that he could emerge the winner in a primary hands down, possibly even forcing the liberals to pull out before the race began.

There was no questioning the fact that Sen. Byrd's blast at the loyalty oath and decision to run as an independent threw the Democrats into a state of alarmed confusion.

Despite the seeming near-glee in liberal quarters that the remaining symbol of the old Byrd Organization had been forced from the party of his fathers, realism quickly began to make itself felt.

In his first reaction to the Byrd decision, State Sen. William B. Hopkins, the Democratic national committeeman, paid tribute to the Byrd legacy of fiscal responsibility but probably alienated much of the Conservative vote when he charged the Senator was "afraid of the people he has not represented".

There was leakage of word that Byrd had rejected importunings from both national and Virginia Republicans that he shift party allegiance. In the aftermath even Gov. Holton expressed regret that the Senator chose the independent course rather than adhering to the two-party system.

Yet there was comfort for the GOP, still exulting over its gubernatorial victory of November 1969. The thinking immediately after the Byrd announcement was that if he takes the Democratic Conservatives with him the July primary likely would be a fiasco, providing Republicans a golden opportunity to capture the seat in November.

Back in January, when asked if and how Byrd could go about recapturing the moderates and even some of the liberals in his own party, Gov. Godwin had stated frankly:

"He will attract the moderates because they will prefer him as a man of integrity, capacity and dedication to what would be an unknown quantity from the liberal fringe. His record has been progressive . . . he's not as ultra-conservative as his father was in his thinking and actions. He has served very responsibly in the Senate and this will be recognized.

"Remember that moderates and conservatives still comprise a large majority of the Democratic Party".

Now, Senator Byrd has charted his own course outside the framework that a new coalition has fashioned for the Democratic Party. It is evident that he expects to attract most of the Conservative elements inside and outside that party, especially the growing numbers of independents.

More or less in control of the state party machinery, the Liberals, with Moderate acquiescence, see the oath as a means of forcing candidate acceptance, if not approval, of the National Democratic Party and any candidates it may nominate.

This poses a difficult problem for many who have spent a lifetime within the State Democratic Party but who followed the leadership of the late Sen. Harry F. Byrd, Sr. in maintaining an aloof or barely tolerating attitude toward the National Party.

It should be obvious what a strain the oath insistence on one hand and the defection of his old friend, Byrd Junior, on the other, has placed on Godwin. Raised in the Byrd Organization, yet advocate of State policies which broke with its traditions, he is bound to feel a great sense of personal trial for his loyalties. His only comfort, if it can be called that, lies in knowing that tens of thousands of fellow Virginians will be faced by the same dilemma.

On the subject of Senator Spong's candidacy for reelection in 1972, Godwin assumes Spong will run and has no plans at all to oppose him.

Well, then, does he have any other political plans?

None at all, really, but he intends to maintain an active interest in both state and national affairs while enjoying a respite from more than two decades of on-and-off campaigning.

When constitutional amendments were being considered at the 1969 special legislative session, Governor Godwin was one of those who poured cold water on the proposal that governors be allowed to seek a second consecutive term.

However, there is no legal roadblock to a governor seeking another term after a four-year period has intervened although this has not been done in this century.

Right now, Godwin truly isn't interested, but of this much we may be certain; four years from now if leaders in his party feel that he alone would be able to oppose the Republican threat successfully he probably would be forced to consider it. Not that he would lay plans or campaign for it but he would not rule out the possibility if the party discovered no other formidable contender. The main problem would be what to do for an encore.

Now that his successor, Governor Holton, has spoken out promptly for the pending constitutional amendments, Mr. Godwin sees bright hope for approval by the people in a nonpartisan campaign and undoubtedly will appear publicly for them if asked.

There is yet another possibility which few have considered for the Godwin talents although it seems a "natural" and this is appointment to a diplomatic post, representing the United States abroad.

The Governor himself appeared surprised when the subject was broached, said he had not been approached, admitted it was an attractive idea but added that everything would have to depend on the type of job. He added emphatically that such an assignment is highly unlikely.

It should be pointed out that Presidents, in recent years at least, frequently have disregarded partisan politics in filling important diplomatic posts. Personal merit and the need to place national interest paramount have brought about better qualified appointments. It would not be a surprise to friends to see Godwin called upon to perform such a related service.

His leading of two Virginia trade missions to Europe not only attracted wide attention but made a lot of friends for Virginia and America. They were wonderful for international un-

derstanding, he declares, and among other things brought a
return three-week visit to Virginia by a Spanish delegation.

Of one thing we may be certain: Mills Godwin is not about
to adopt permanently the retired country gentleman way of life.
He simply isn't built that way.

And Over Here, Senoras and Senors, we have . . . . *Governor Godwin
shows Valenzuela family, his hosts when he was in Spain, around the
gallery of past governors outside his office. Gov. J. Lindsey Almond, Jr.
looks on from portrait.*

—Richmond Newspapers Photo

196

LOOKING BACKWARD

No man of true leadership and ability ever comes to the close of a major effort without wondering if he could have done better or without looking backward to remember in gratitude those who helped him to success.

Thus, it was a grateful Mills Godwin who sat with the author one afternoon in the library of the Mansion and sought to assess his blessings.

"I could not end these four years without paying tribute to the people of this Commonwealth for their part in helping to get things done—to their understanding, cooperation and loyalty", he mused.

"Virginians are good to their governors, particularly to me. They have tolerated my faults, they have been ever willing to overlook my shortcomings and they have taken much on faith in the approach to trying to solve some of our problems.

"They have been willing to accept tax burdens that have been substantially increased in the hope that State services would be commensurate with the investment they were making.

"Then, there has been my wonderful relationship with the General Assembly—it has been one of the sheer delights of my term as Governor. No Governor in my memory—and, from what I have been told, in anyone's memory—has enjoyed a finer relationship.

"Every major legislative proposal I made has been enacted into law. The only exception of any significance was my recommendation for lowering the blood alcoholic content for drunken driving from 0.15 to 0.10 per cent. It was changed to 'impaired driving' with lesser penalty. In the public interest, I have recommended it again in my final message to the Assembly.

"I attribute this success to real understanding that existed between the leadership of the two houses and the Governor's office—a mutual trust and confidence that we enjoyed and a knowledge of the responsibilities of each. This is vastly important to any successful administration".

He mentioned especially Lt. Gov. Fred G. Pollard and House Speaker John Warren Cooke as well as committee chairmen.

There was warm tribute, too, for the members of his personal staff during those four years:

"By anybody's standards, Carter O. Lowance, my commissioner of administration, is one of Virginia's great public servants. His advice, his guidance and his loyalty are beyond any praise I can give. He's just a genuinely fine individual with a real awareness of his responsibilities".

John H. Wessells, chief press representative, and Mrs. Pat Perkinson, administrative assistant who had been with him since the 1965 campaign, he described glowingly as "diligent, faithful, capable, loyal and dedicated".

There was praise, too, for Archie L. Yeatts, whom he moved to the ABC Board and to Bruce Y. Miller, as well as for the two confidential secretaries, Mrs. Audrey S. Moore and Mrs. Patty W. Fowler. Mrs. Moore had been with him five years and Mrs. Fowler was a holdover from Governor Harrison's staff.

Last Christmas With the Staff and friends: In usual order, Lowance, Perkinson, Fowler, Lee, Sen. Lloyd Bird, Councill, the Governor, Sen. Paul Manns, Curry, Millancote, Bruce Miller, Wilson, Abbot, Wessells and Prendergast.

"Their dedication has made for whatever success this administration has enjoyed", he said, speaking of them collectively.

He thought of the two thousand or more men and women he had appointed to leading departmental posts, to the regulatory and policy boards and to the boards of visitors of state colleges and institutions.

"I have been continually impressed with the available caliber of the men and women who have been willing to give of their time, effort and talent without pay. Few refuse the Governor's call to service".

He never ceased to be amazed at the eagerness with which so many sought appointment as visitors to all state institutions, but especially to the "Big Four", in the order of age, William and Mary, the University of Virginia, Virginia Military Institute and Virginia Polytechnic Institute. Alumni of VMI he described as the most persistent.

Godwin, like Gov. Albertis S. Harrison, Jr. before him, deliberately discontinued the practice of naming legislators to college boards, feeling that they tended to be too partisan and therefore lacking in objectivity when money requests of their schools, in particular, were before the Assembly.

In general, he tried to stick to recommendation lists from alumni associations which submit two or three names for each vacancy.

Realistically, he confesses that all appointments involve wielding of great political power and as such have their political effect.

The loneliness that often accompanys life in the Mansion can be offset only by keeping constantly busy or in having some close friends whose frequent presence, especially when needed, plays a part in bringing relaxation.

Godwin remembered especially former Delegate Shirley T. Holland and his wife, Gladys, from Isle of Wight. Holland with 20 years in the House, he called "my political ally and greatest booster", a man who served as his liaison with the General Assembly during the 1966 and 1968 sessions and whose help he called "very effective".

Mentioned, too, were the Edward E. Lanes of Richmond, like the Hollands frequent guests at the Mansion, at Camp

Pendleton or on other trips. There were also the A. Gordon Brooks, whose devotion has been mentioned, Dr. and Mrs. Herbert C. Lee and, of course, Lowance and his wife, Elizabeth.

Both Godwin and his First Lady had praise and kind words for the Mansion staff "who looked after our every need and were always kind and considerate".

The Mansion Staff: Seated, Beatrice Bailey, Alease Elam and Lucille Anderson; Standing, Tom Bannister, Pearl Hockaday, Raymond Wilson. Missing when picture was taken in January 1970 shortly before Godwin left office, was Bernice Williams.

It was a display of gratitude to the butlers, Thomas Bannister and Raymond Wilson, that the Governor spent part of his last full day in office fulfilling their long-time ambition to take a flight in one of the State planes.

The pleasure they derived from the experience was thanks enough.

Another demonstration of the warm nature of the Godwins was that, in departing, they left not only a spotless and shining

Mansion but a personal gift for each of the incoming Holton family from Governor to his youngest child.

Godwin recalled the many personal relationships with legislators who had supported him on such things as the sales tax, some at considerable risk, and for whom he had cut electronic campaign tapes or made local appearences in acknowledgement of their courage.

There was pride in his voice at the fact that this had helped make him the leader of his party and he recalled that in 1967 they had made him the speaker for the Jefferson-Jackson Day dinner, an honor almost always conferred on an outsider, preferably a national leader.

No, there was nothing much he would have done differently and the only big regret is that he could not have done more.

As he told Guy Friddell, editorial page editor of the Norfolk Virginian-Pilot:

"I was maybe the right Governor—and I put 'maybe' before that—but certainly I appeared on the scene at the right time. The people of Virginia were ready to move. If I made any valid assumption, it was in 1964 and 1965 that Virginia's climate of public opinion was ready for progress. And the people are still ready for reasonable progress.

"I shall enjoy the opportunity to watch it, and I hope that others have a good measure of success in what they try to do; and, just as I have, they will find that they won't get it all done".

Godwin undoubtedly enjoyed the "best press" of any governor in a long time. He may not have had the old-shoe ease of a Bill Tuck with a store of homespun stories ready for quick tapping but he was always affable, approachable and helpful.

When he went too long without a press conference, it was possible for Capitol Hill reporters to slip in the back door. In the words of one veteran newsman—they prefer not to be quoted lest they be thought partial—"he was always his own best press agent—he cultivated the press with calculation and coolness but with mutually good results that added to the public's available information on Virginia politics and government".

It was with this news sense that he prepared for his press conference on the last day of 1969 a list of what he considered the 10 top stories of his tenure.

Here they are in the order he saw them so that future historians may judge:

- Passage of the $81 million bond issue.
- Enactment of the sales tax, earmarked for education.
- Unparalleled prosperity.
- Growing role of black citizens in business and public life.
- Establishment of the Community College system and upgrading education at all levels.
- Progress of the nine-year highway program.
- Attacks on social and environmental problems.
- Movement toward constitutional revision.
- Hurricane Camille's awesome toll of life and property.
- Passage of local option liquor-by-the-drink legislation.

Camille, which hit August 20-21, 1969, was a natural disaster, of course, and Godwin's part was to help coordinate relief and restoration. During the hours and days immediately following, he was a symbol of the concern of all Virginians.

Liquor-by-the-drink was not one of his projects, despite its far-reaching effect, and hardly will play any part in future assessment of the Godwin story.

It is by the long range effect of controlled events that Mills E. Godwin's place in history will be determined. Repeating his observation in the preface to these pages, the author believes that the Governor's monument will rest on a three-tiered solid base:

- End of the pay-as-you-go system through passage of the sales tax and the $81 million bond issue.
- Establishment of the Community College system and the major forward thrust of both public and higher education.
- Remarkable industrial development of the State.

Together they comprise an era of unmatched brilliance.

HAIL AND FAREWELL

During his four-year tenure, each Governor of Virginia is intimately associated with three biennial budgets but, oddly enough, only in the case of the mid-term budget does he have complete control. Even then, the last six months of its effectiveness come under his successor.

His first budget has been prepared by his predecessor and although he may lead the way in certain changes by the General Assembly, as did Mills Godwin with the sales tax, he is usually compelled to follow the financial course set by another.

His last budget, prepared during his final year in office, does not become effective until six months after his term ends and can be altered by the General Assembly at the insistence of his successor.

Yet, this system has meant stability to Virginia government and attempts to change it in favor of annual budgets have been unavailing. Even the pending constitutional amendments which provide for annual sessions are hardly likely to revise the system.

Godwin, who together with Budget Director L. M. Kuhn and the legislative advisory and business advisory commissions, prepared the budget in effect until June 30, 1970 and projected the one for the July 1, 1970-June 30, 1972 biennium, would have it no other way.

"I know of no single thing a governor does which is as important as budget-making. He has the constitutional duty to present to the General Assembly a budget based on revenues estimated to be available in the next biennium and the appropriations showing the other side of the picture. He is under mandate to balance it.

"Fortunately, he possesses the line item veto power. He also has control over the release of funds not only for maintenance and operation but for capital outlay. He must be able to certify that the money is there".

Virginia's budget has risen every biennium for decades— not a sign of extravagance but of growth. Yet, due to the conservative influence of Harry F. Byrd, each governor tried consciously to leave a surplus. This was accomplished by deliberately underestimating revenue.

Thanks to raising of income tax rates under Governor Tuck, the first large surplus ($70 million) was experienced under Governor Battle and was appropriated to aid school construction in the localities, thus breaking a time-honored rule.

The $103 million surplus estimated by Governor Harrison for June 30, 1966 in Godwin's term proved to be only $83 million, consequently there was some belt-tightening. The amount was considerably less midway of the Godwin term in 1968. That helped sell the idea of bonds for capital improvements.

Starting work on the 1970-72 budget in the spring of 1969, Godwin was well aware that every cent would be needed to operate the expanded programs he had put through, despite the conceded 8 per cent annual economic growth of the State.

Thus it was that the budget given the General Assembly on Friday, January 16—his last full day in office—was a "tight" one despite its record $3.8 billion figure that used all of an estimated $84 million surplus and left only $1 million for Governor Holton and the legislators "to play with".

Godwin's projections allowed only $25.5 million for capital outlay at institutions despite requests exceeding $300 million. Additional building, he said, would have to wait for amendment of the Constitution with more extensive borrowing powers.

There was provision for a 10 per cent across-the-board pay boost for 50,000 state employes and $300 increases for teachers in each year of the biennium.

He made no provision for $40 million annually estimated necessary to carry out Holton's pet campaign project of giving taxpayers a $9 per year refund for sales tax on food.

The budget also carried huge increases for public schools and higher education as well as mental health. And, because he had to, Godwin put in $57.5 million to help get Medicaid started with federal matching funds while boosting welfare funds 42 per cent.

In addition, although he could admit it was not enough, there was more money to aid in expansion of water resources as well as develop air pollution control which he had initiated. There

204

likewise was a moderate ($2.7 million) recommendation to help get started on putting port facilities under a single authority.

And just so he would not be accused of "padding" one way or the other, he observed:

"The estimates on which this budget is based are the most liberal of my four years as Governor and the 22 years I have been in Virginia's government. They stretch to the limit the best judgment of our own fiscal officers and outstanding advisors from business, industry and banking throughout the State. I am convinced that to push the estimates higher would be not only unsound but would border on irresponsibility".

This was almost anti-climactic, however, compared to Governor Godwin's final address in leave-taking of the General Assembly when the 1970 session convened two days before on January 14.

The greeting extended him by House and Senate, meeting jointly, was one of the most rousing within memory of long-time observers of the Capitol scene. It was a proud moment and his were not the only misty eyes as he strode to the lectern to make his accounting of four years of stewardship.

"Politics", he told them, "can be a balky servant or a tyrannical master, and yet the intangible rewards of public service continue to attract men and women of great ability. During the four years of this administration, the members of this body and countless Virginians from every walk of life have come forward, as eager volunteers, to assume a portion of our labors".

The early 1960's, he said, had provided a period of calm in which to heal the scars of strife which had "struck at the very taproot of our society and threatened public support of education".

"During those years, peace, rather than progress, was the prayer of many people. And yet, as the decade advanced, the footings were quietly poured for a better day", he added, proceeding to sketch the remarkable changes of 1966-70 with which we have dealt more fully in the preceding chapters.

A realist looking to the future, Godwin was frank to say:

"Just as I reaped where a predecessor had sown, so will the full results of this administration be measured by someone else".

Predicting doubled college enrollments in a decade ahead,

he warned that only new revenue sources can build the colleges, the highways and the hospitals while cleaning the streams and the air. Final approval of the constitutional amendments, so nobly begun, he held a necessity to that progress.

With pride he could remind Virginians that theirs was the only National Guard between Boston and Miami on the Atlantic Seaboard which had not been called out to prevent civil disobedience. Credit he gave to the basic soundness of the people and to a firm use of State Police when necessary. Increasing their number by 50 to a total of 1,000 in the next two years he regarded as justified. Judging by the applause, so did the Assembly.

"Slowly, often painfully, we have learned that we cannot keep on doing things in the same old ways, and yet the new ways are not clearly in focus", he asserted.

Warning that Virginians remain basically conservative, he took issue with the feeling of some that the November election events marked a major change in philosophical direction.

"The truth is, they merely affirm once more that while our people may, at times, change their labels in the polling booths, they do not radically change their views", he said.

And so saying, he closed out his administration with words remindful of its beginning:

"Whatever the clamor of the moment, in the long run, *Virginia's future rests on the twin pillars of jobs and education.* They alone will bring an end to our frustrations. They alone will give our people something to defend, rather than something to demand. . . .

"Virginia's greatest years are not behind us, but ahead of us . . ."

But none who has witnessed what has gone before could deny that the four years so many have saluted as "The Godwin Years" deserve to rank among the greatest in the long and proud story of the Old Dominion.

The time was ripe for change when he at last came to the governorship along a well-charted course to find the people ready and eager for progress, waiting only for the right leadership.

Every governor, whatever his state, comes to office with a program and high hopes, but all too few possess the necessary combination of political know-how, personal charm and genuine persuasiveness with both voters and politicians which can turn plans into reality.

History will record Mills E. Godwin, Jr. as an extraordinary achiever—a Virginian for his time—but when the final chapter is written his fame is likely to rest on the fact that he truly awakened a great State to its full potential.

There is still more to be done!

207